■ SCHOLASTIC

Quilt
Math

by Cindi Mitchell

Miss Cheng

New York • Toronto • London • Auckland • Sydney
Mexico City • New Delhi • Hong Kong • Buenos Aires

Teaching *Resources*

This book is dedicated to the amazing women in my quilt group. They have shown me how to use the latest quilting tools and create a perfect triangle with fabric, but their greatest lessons have been about giving, sharing, and loving. They make more than 150 quilts a year to donate to local charities.

Cover design by Brian LaRossa
Interior design and illustrations by Cindi, Ben, and Jim Mitchell

ISBN: 0-439-38533-4
Copyright © 2005 by Cindi Mitchell
Published by Scholastic Inc.
All rights reserved.
Printed in U.S.A.

1 2 3 4 5 6 7 8 9 10   40   13 12 11 10 09 08 07 06 05

Contents

Continued

Introduction

The tradition of quilting has been passed down in my family for generations. My mother is a quilter, and so was my grandmother, great grandmother, and great-great grandmother! I learned to sew at a young age, and I was also taught to appreciate the fine art of creating and preserving quilts.

In my family, I have the awesome responsibility of being the "keeper of the quilts." I have new and old family quilts everywhere. They are hung on rods in my living room, placed over banisters, and tucked away in cupboards. Some quilts are so old and tattered that we have taken pieces of them and preserved them inside picture frames.

A few months ago, we had to evacuate our home for a hurricane. I packed our car with our most important possessions to get ready to leave town. First, I packed the old family quilts and our picture albums. There was almost no space left for anything else.

My daughter came out to the car with her load of favorite possessions. On the top of her stack was a quilt her grandmother had made and a baby quilt given to her by her aunt, Marianne. I am glad that my daughter treasures quilts and the time-honored tradition of quilting as much as I do.

As your students work on the quilt block activity pages in this book, I hope that they learn to appreciate the wonderful art of quilting, too.

How to Use This Book

Each reproducible activity page in this book has three parts:

◆ Math Skill See at a glance the math skill focus of the activity.

◆ Quilt Block Each quilt block design contains math problems for students to solve. After completing all of the math problems, students color their quilt block using the key near the bottom of the page as a guide. Reading the key gives students practice in following directions and additional practice in math. Students will need a 16-pack of crayons or colored pencils to color their quilt blocks.

◆ Extra! This extension activity reinforces the math skill or relates to the geometry of the quilt block on the page. Invite students to complete this section after they have finished coloring the quilt block. Answers can be found on page 110.

Once students have completed the activity pages, consider making a Collaborative Quilt Art display in your classroom. Simply mount each quilt block on a square of construction paper and place the squares together on a bulletin board.

The last two activities in the book (pages 108–109) give students the opportunity to create their own quilt block designs. But don't stop here! Challenge your students further by trying some of the Taking It Further activities on the next page.

Taking It Further

✂— Give each student a handful of pattern blocks and a sheet of 1-inch grid paper. Ask students to create a quilt block on the grid paper using any three pattern blocks.

✂— Give each student one pattern block triangle to trace on a sheet of grid paper. Then challenge students to create a quilt block using only that size triangle. Direct them to center their pattern on the grid. Then tell them that they may flip or turn the triangle to create their design. Afterward, invite them to color and name their quilt block.

✂— Invite each student to design a quilt block on grid paper using three different shapes. One of the shapes must be an octagon.

✂— Encourage each student to design a picture quilt block that depicts an event in his or her life. Have students cut the picture-block shapes out of different colors of construction paper and glue them onto a background square of construction paper. Then, place the squares together on a wall to make a class quilt.

✂— Let students research quilt block patterns in books or on the Internet. Have them reproduce on grid paper some of the patterns they find.

✂— Encourage each student to design a quilt block that has one or more lines of symmetry, as shown on the quilt blocks at right.

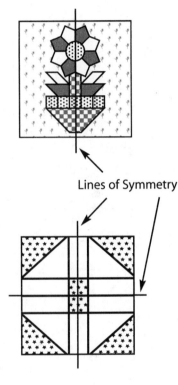

Lines of Symmetry

Suggested Resources

Web Site

Quilts and Quiltmaking in America 1978-1976
http://memory.loc.gov/ammem/qlthtml/qlthome.html
This website from the Library of Congress offers photographs of hundreds of quilts along with information about the people who made them.

Books

Quilt-Block History of Pioneer Days, by Mary Cobb (The Millbrook Press, 1995). This delightful book tells the history of the pioneer days through quilts. It includes pictures of dozens of quilt blocks and information about them, as well as projects that kids can make.

Traditional Quilts for Kids to Make, by Barbara J. Eikmeier (The Patchwork Place, 2001). This book includes eight traditional quilt plans and 15 traditional blocks designed especially for children to make. It teaches quiltmaking basics from choosing fabrics to using a sewing machine, to rotary cutting and hand-quilting.

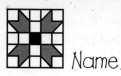

Name_____

David and Goliath

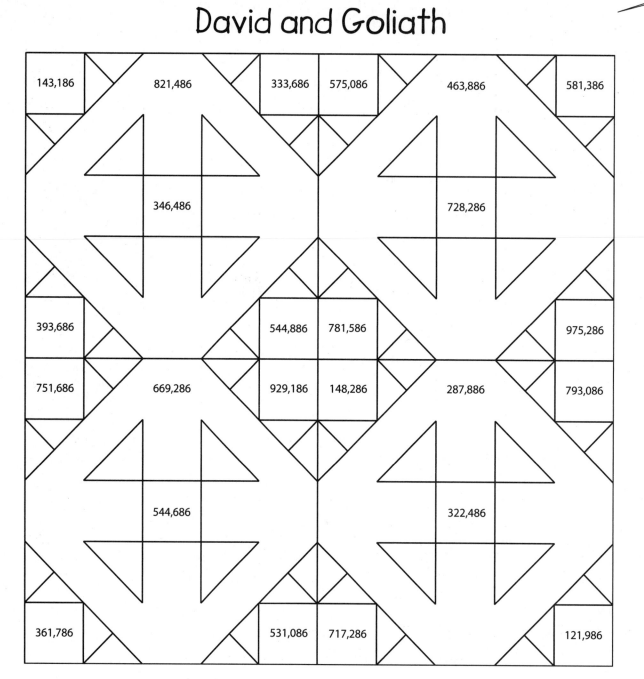

143,186   821,486   333,686   575,086   463,886   581,386

346,486   728,286

393,686   544,886   781,586   975,286

751,686   669,286   929,186   148,286   287,886   793,086

544,686   322,486

361,786   531,086   717,286   121,986

Look at each number.

If the number in the	Color the shape
hundred thousands place is even	black
ten thousands place is odd	green
thousands place is even	purple
hundreds place is odd	yellow

Fill in the other shapes with colors of your choice.

Extra! On the back of this page, write the number that is one less than 10,000,000.

8

Rosebud

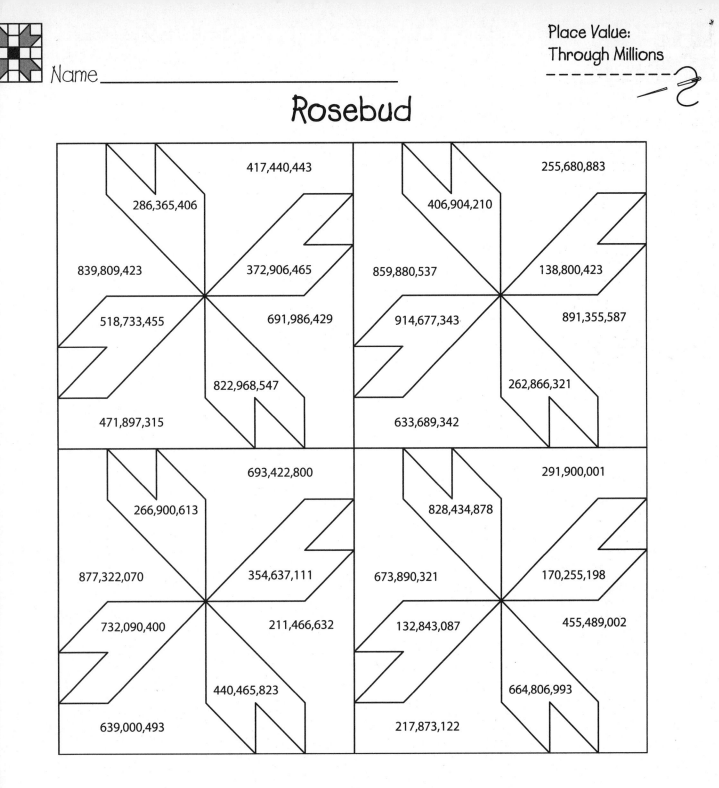

417,440,443

286,365,406

839,809,423   372,906,465

518,733,455   691,986,429

822,968,547

471,897,315

255,680,883

406,904,210

859,880,537   138,800,423

914,677,343   891,355,587

262,866,321

633,689,342

693,422,800

266,900,613

877,322,070   354,637,111

732,090,400   211,466,632

440,465,823

639,000,493

291,900,001

828,434,878

673,890,321   170,255,198

132,843,087   455,489,002

664,806,993

217,873,122

Look at each number.

If the number in the	Color the shape
hundred millions place is odd	red
ten millions place is even	pink
millions place is odd	green

 On the back of this page, write the number that is ten million more than 45,000.

9

Name_____

Aunt Eliza's Star

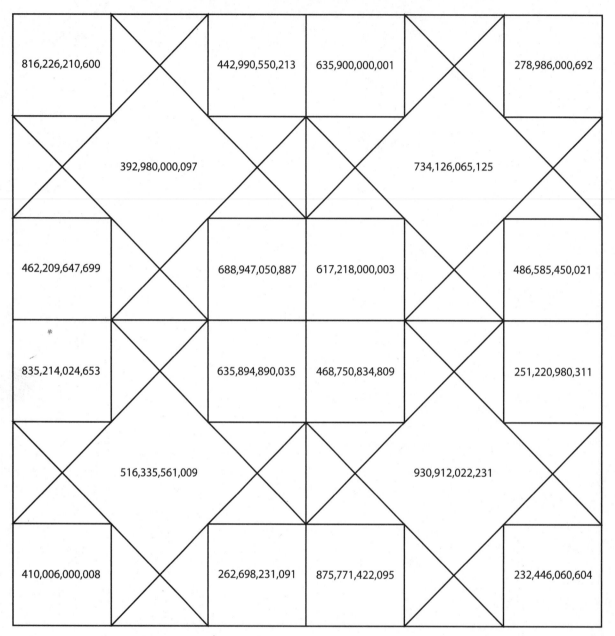

816,226,210,600

442,990,550,213   635,900,000,001

278,986,000,692

392,980,000,097

734,126,065,125

462,209,647,699

688,947,050,887   617,218,000,003

486,585,450,021

835,214,024,653

635,894,890,035   468,750,834,809

251,220,980,311

516,335,561,009

930,912,022,231

410,006,000,008

262,698,231,091   875,771,422,095

232,446,060,604

Look at each number.

If the number in the	Color the shape
hundred billions place is odd	yellow
ten billions place is even	dark green
billions place is odd	dark blue
ones place is even	orange

Fill in the other shapes with colors of your choice.

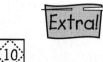 **Extra!** On the back of this page, write the number that is one less than *one hundred billion* in numeral form.

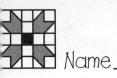

Name_____

Annie's Choice

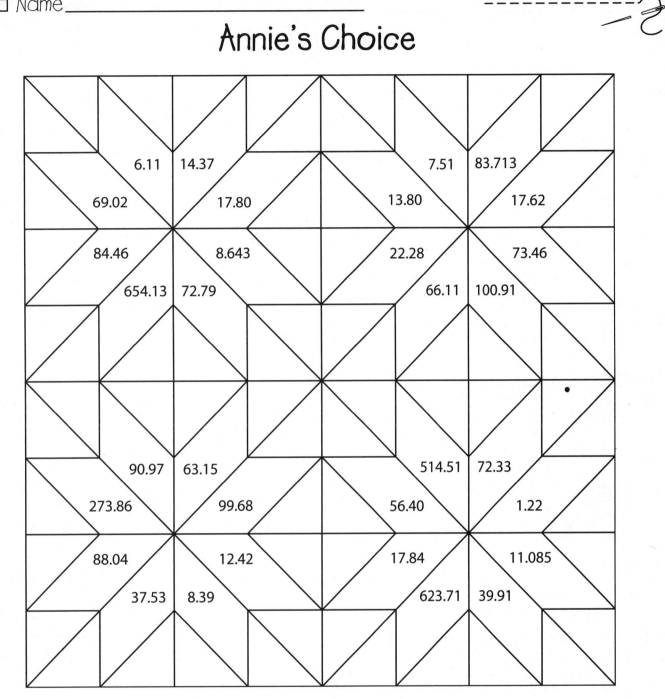

6.11 | 14.37 | 7.51 | 83.713
69.02 | 17.80 | 13.80 | 17.62
84.46 | 8.643 | 22.28 | 73.46
654.13 | 72.79 | 66.11 | 100.91
90.97 | 63.15 | 514.51 | 72.33
273.86 | 99.68 | 56.40 | 1.22
88.04 | 12.42 | 17.84 | 11.085
37.53 | 8.39 | 623.71 | 39.91

Look at each number.

If the number in the	Color the shape
tenths place is odd	red
hundredths place is even	dark blue

Fill in the other shapes with colors of your choice.

 Extra! On the back of this page, write the number *twenty-three and ninety-five hundredths* in decimal form.

Name_____

French Star

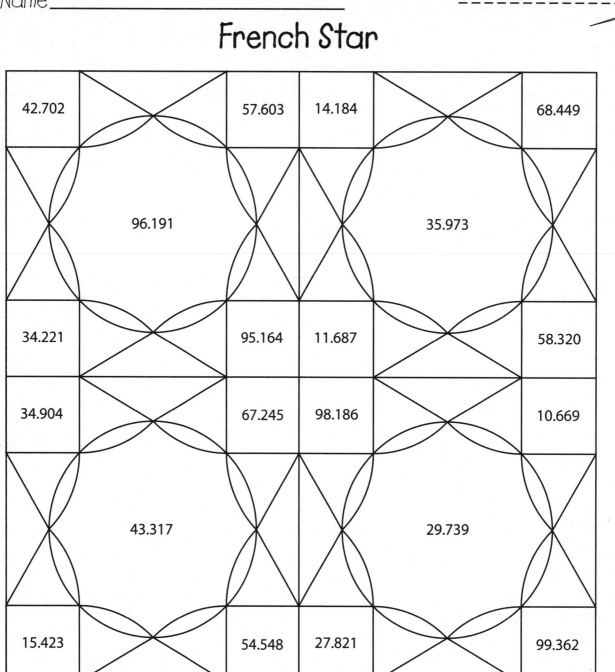

42.702		57.603	14.184		68.449
96.191			35.973		
34.221		95.164	11.687		58.320
34.904		67.245	98.186		10.669
43.317			29.739		
15.423		54.548	27.821		99.362

Look at each number.

If the number in the	Color the shape
tenths place is even	red
hundredths place is odd	orange
thousandths place is even	yellow

Fill in the other shapes with colors of your choice.

Quilt Math: Grades 4–6 Scholastic Teaching Resources

Extra! On the back of this page, write the decimal *fourteen and two thousandths* in decimal form.

12

Name _____

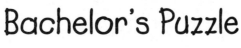

Bachelor's Puzzle

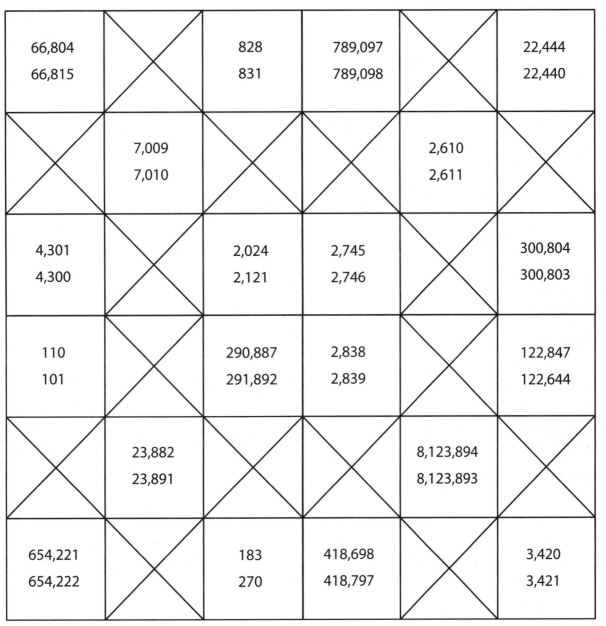

66,804 66,815		828 831	789,097 789,098		22,444 22,440
	7,009 7,010			2,610 2,611	
4,301 4,300		2,024 2,121	2,745 2,746		300,804 300,803
110 101		290,887 291,892	2,838 2,839		122,847 122,644
	23,882 23,891			8,123,894 8,123,893	
654,221 654,222		183 270	418,698 418,797		3,420 3,421

Compare the numbers in each shape.

If the greater number is	Color the shape
odd	orange
even	dark blue

Fill in the other
shapes with
colors of your
choice.

Extra! On the back of this page, write any five-digit number. Then, write the numbers that are ten greater than and ten less than this number.

Name_____

Green Mountain Star

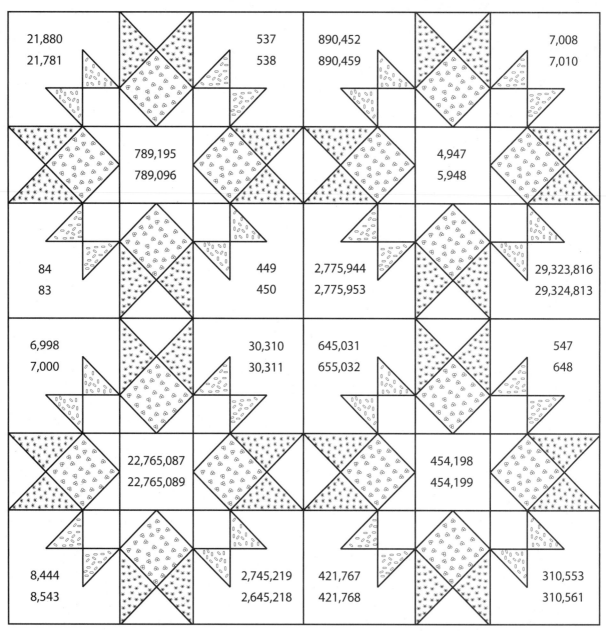

| 21,880 | | | 537 | 890,452 | | | 7,008 |
| 21,781 | | | 538 | 890,459 | | | 7,010 |

| | 789,195 | | | | 4,947 | | |
| | 789,096 | | | | 5,948 | | |

| 84 | | | 449 | 2,775,944 | | | 29,323,816 |
| 83 | | | 450 | 2,775,953 | | | 29,324,813 |

| 6,998 | | | 30,310 | 645,031 | | | 547 |
| 7,000 | | | 30,311 | 655,032 | | | 648 |

| | 22,765,087 | | | | 454,198 | | |
| | 22,765,089 | | | | 454,199 | | |

| 8,444 | | | 2,745,219 | 421,767 | | | 310,553 |
| 8,543 | | | 2,645,218 | 421,768 | | | 310,561 |

Compare the numbers in each shape.

If the lesser number is	Color the shape
odd	green
even	yellow

Fill in the other shapes with colors of your choice.

Extra! On the back of this page, write the largest number possible using the following digits: 0, 4, 3, 9, 9, 1, 6.

Quilt Math: Grades 4–6 Scholastic Teaching Resources

Name_____

Brave World

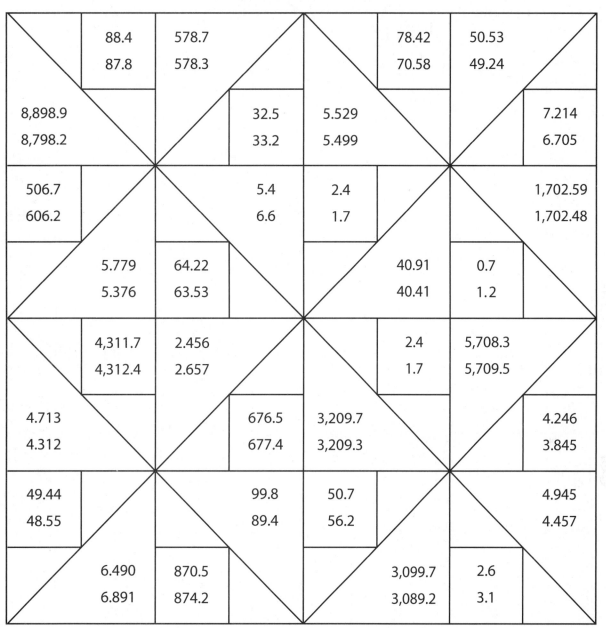

88.4 87.8	578.7 578.3		78.42 70.58	50.53 49.24	
8,898.9 8,798.2		32.5 33.2	5.529 5.499		7.214 6.705
506.7 606.2		5.4 6.6	2.4 1.7		1,702.59 1,702.48
5.779 5.376	64.22 63.53		40.91 40.41	0.7 1.2	
4,311.7 4,312.4	2.456 2.657		2.4 1.7	5,708.3 5,709.5	
4.713 4.312		676.5 677.4	3,209.7 3,209.3		4.246 3.845
49.44 48.55		99.8 89.4	50.7 56.2		4.945 4.457
6.490 6.891	870.5 874.2		3,099.7 3,089.2	2.6 3.1	

Compare the numbers in each shape.

If the greater number	Color the shape
rounds up to the nearest whole number	red
rounds down to the nearest whole number	blue

Fill in the other shapes with colors of your choice.

 Extra! On the back of this page, write the number 38.05. Then, write the numbers that are one-tenth greater and one-tenth less than this number.

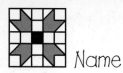

Name_____

Bird of Paradise

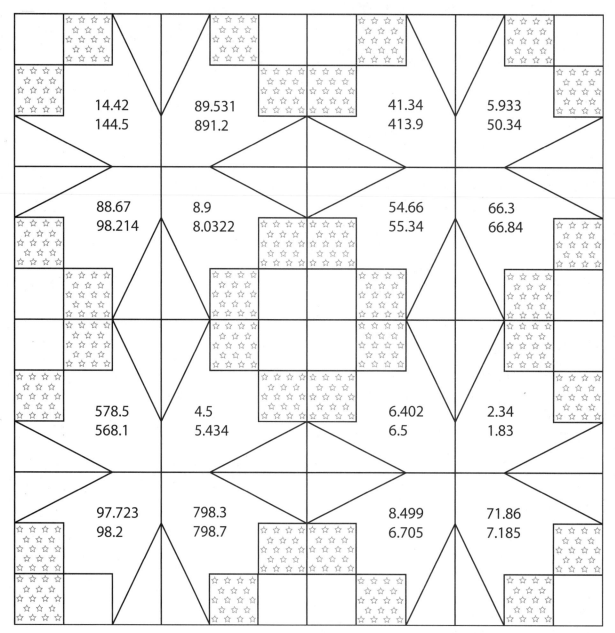

14.42
144.5

89.531
891.2

41.34
413.9

5.933
50.34

88.67
98.214

8.9
8.0322

54.66
55.34

66.3
66.84

578.5
568.1

4.5
5.434

6.402
6.5

2.34
1.83

97.723
98.2

798.3
798.7

8.499
6.705

71.86
7.185

Compare the numbers in each shape.

If the greater number	Color the shape
rounds up to the nearest whole number	purple
rounds down to the nearest whole number	green

Fill in the other shapes with colors of your choice.

 • On the back of this page, write the following numbers in order from least to greatest: 12.4, 12.04, 12.44, 12.06.

16

Name _____

Balkan Puzzle

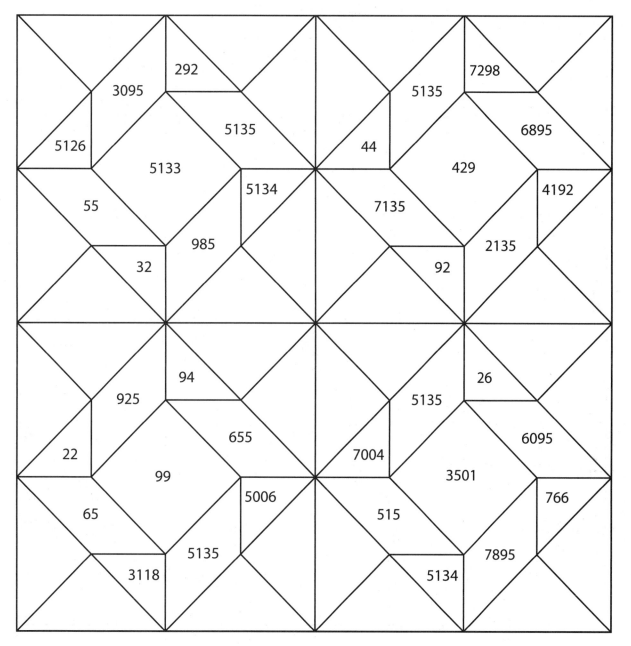

3095 292 7298
5135
5135
5126 6895
5133 44
5134 429 4192
55 7135
985 2135
32 92
94 26
925 5135
655 6095
22 7004
99 3501
65 5006 766
515
5135 7895
3118 5134

Look at each number.

If the number is	Color the shape
divisible by 2	blue
divisible by 3	orange
divisible by 5	green

Fill in the other shapes with colors of your choice.

 On the back of this page, write the smallest number that is divisible by 2, 5, and 3.

17

Name_____

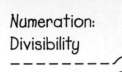
Box Pattern

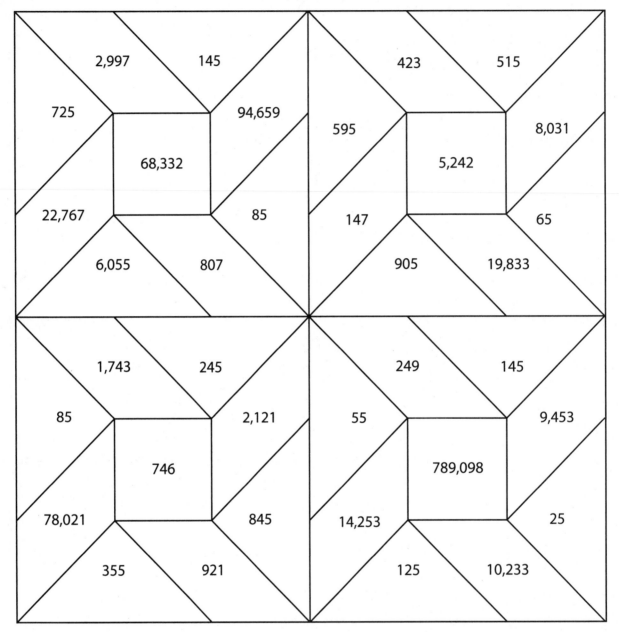

Look at each number.

If the number is	Color the shape
divisible by 2	yellow
divisible by 3	purple
divisible by 5	pink

Fill in the other shapes with colors of your choice.

Extra! If a number is divisible by 10, is it also divisible by 2? Explain your answer on the back of this page.

18

Name _____

Road to Tennessee

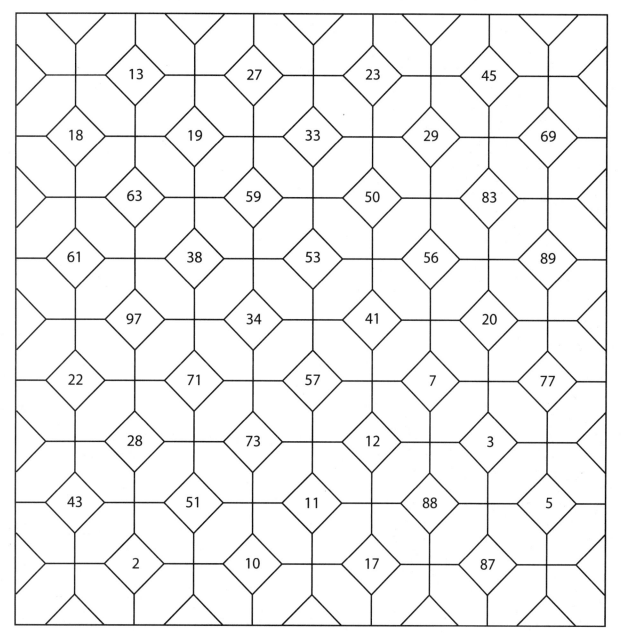

13   27   23   45

18   19   33   29   69

63   59   50   83

61   38   53   56   89

97   34   41   20

22   71   57   7   77

28   73   12   3

43   51   11   88   5

2   10   17   87

Look at each number.

If the number is	Color the shape
prime	red
composite	black

Fill in the other shapes with colors of your choice.

 On the back of this page, write the eight prime numbers that are less than 20.

Name_____

Blazing Star

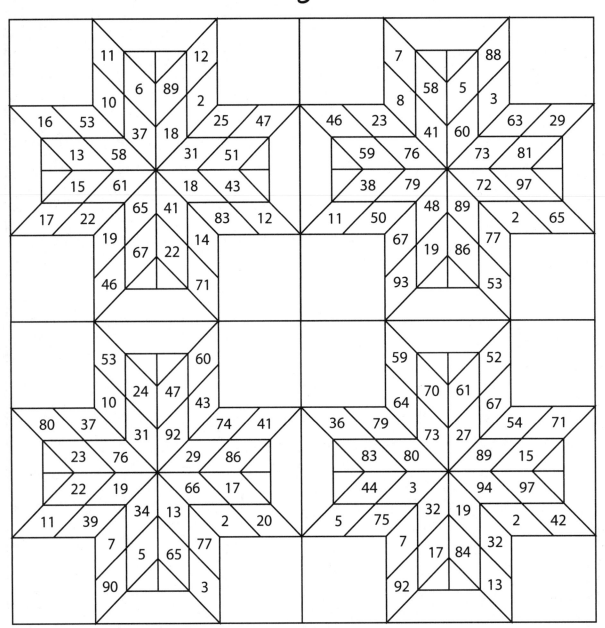

Look at each number.

If the number is	Color the shape
prime	red
composite	black

Fill in the other shapes with colors of your choice.

Extra! • Circle the number that is prime:

27   13   18   33   72

20

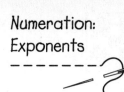

Waste Not

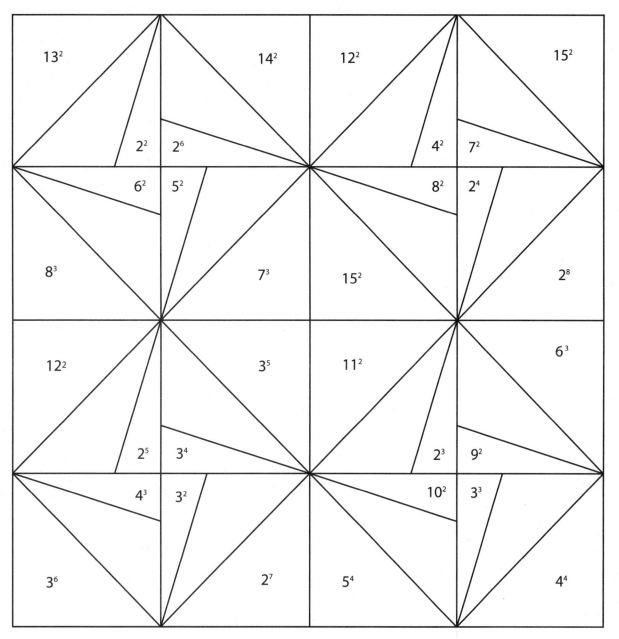

Name _____

Within the quilt grid:

13^2 14^2 12^2 15^2

2^2 2^6 4^2 7^2

6^2 5^2 8^2 2^4

8^3 7^3 15^2 2^8

12^2 3^5 11^2 6^3

2^5 3^4 2^3 9^2

4^3 3^2 10^2 3^3

3^6 2^7 5^4 4^4

Write each number in standard form.

If the answer is between	Color the shape
2 and 35	red
36 and 100	pink
101 and 730	green

Fill in the other
shapes with
colors of your
choice.

Extra! What is the greatest exponent with a base of 2 that gives a product less than 100?
Write your answer on the back of this page.

Name_____

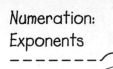

Bow Ties

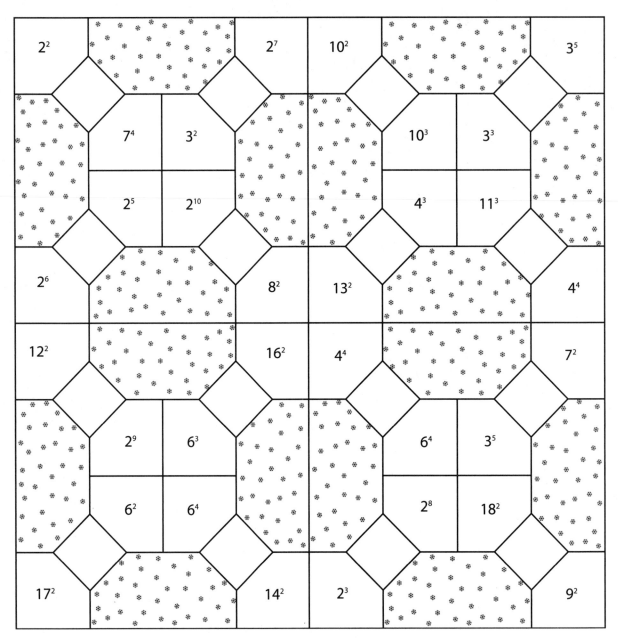

Write each number in standard form.

If the number is between	Color the shape
1 and 300	red
301 to 2000	gray

Fill in the other
shapes with
colors of your
choice.

Extra! On the back of this page, write in exponential form: 8 x 8 x 8 x 8 x 8.

22

Name _____

Castor and Pollux

On each line below, write the name of a color you like best.
Then look at each number.

If the number is	Color the shape
even	_____
odd	_____

Fill in the other shapes with colors of your choice.

 Extra! • If you add two odd numbers, is the answer odd or even? Give an example.
Write your answer on the back of this page.

Name_____

Judy of Arabia

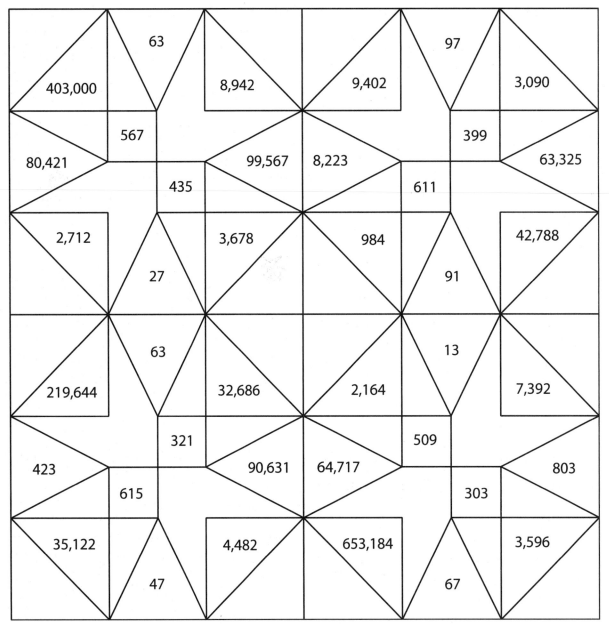

Look at each number.

If the number	Color the shape
is even	pink
is odd	green

Fill in the other shapes with colors of your choice.

Extra! • If you add two even numbers, is the answer odd or even? Give an example. Write your answer on the back of this page.

Name _____

Clown

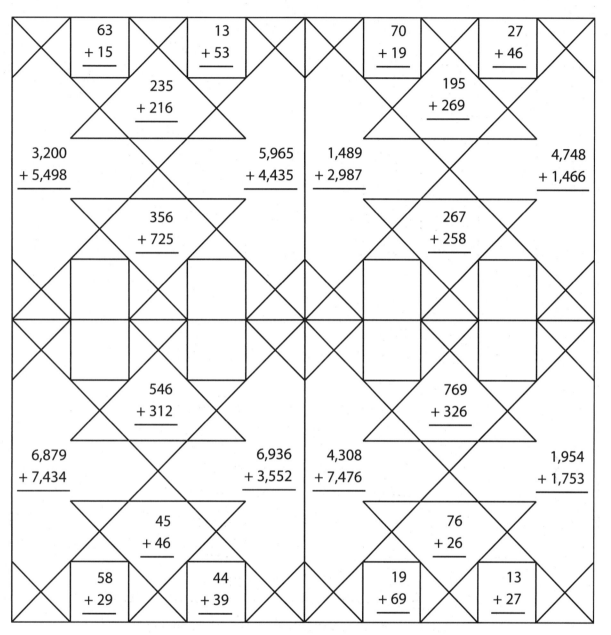

$$63 + 15$$ $$13 + 53$$ $$70 + 19$$ $$27 + 46$$

$$235 + 216$$ $$195 + 269$$

$$3,200 + 5,498$$ $$5,965 + 4,435$$ $$1,489 + 2,987$$ $$4,748 + 1,466$$

$$356 + 725$$ $$267 + 258$$

$$546 + 312$$ $$769 + 326$$

$$6,879 + 7,434$$ $$6,936 + 3,552$$ $$4,308 + 7,476$$ $$1,954 + 1,753$$

$$45 + 46$$ $$76 + 26$$

$$58 + 29$$ $$44 + 39$$ $$19 + 69$$ $$13 + 27$$

Round each number to the greatest place value.
Then estimate the sum.

If the sum is between	Color the shape
0 to 90	dark orange
100 to 500	yellow
600 to 1,200	light orange
1,300 to 20,000	blue

Fill in the other
shapes with
colors of your
choice.

Extra! On the back of this page, write two addition problems that each have estimated
sums of 4,000.

25

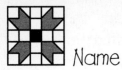

Name _____

Stained-Glass Window

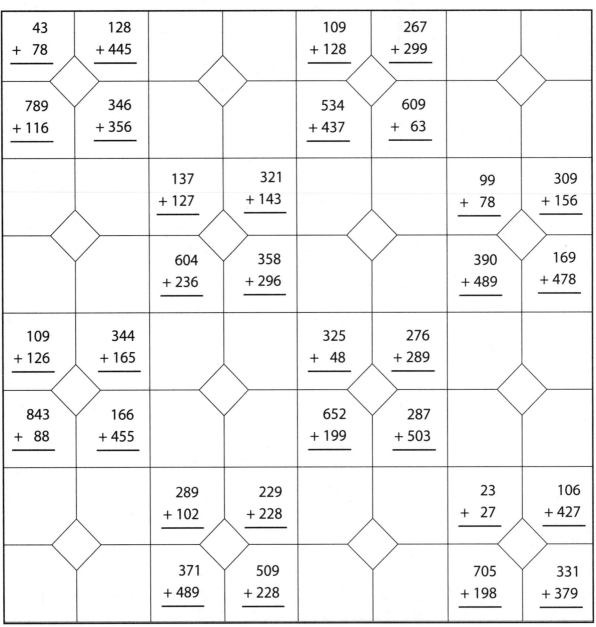

43 + 78	128 + 445			109 + 128	267 + 299	
789 + 116	346 + 356			534 + 437	609 + 63	
		137 + 127	321 + 143			99 + 78	309 + 156
		604 + 236	358 + 296			390 + 489	169 + 478
109 + 126	344 + 165			325 + 48	276 + 289	
843 + 88	166 + 455			652 + 199	287 + 503	
		289 + 102	229 + 228			23 + 27	106 + 427
		371 + 489	509 + 228			705 + 198	331 + 379

Solve the problems.

If the sum is between	Color the shape
1 and 420	yellow
421 and 620	red
621 and 820	blue
821 and 1000	green

Fill in the other shapes with colors of your choice.

Extra! On the back of this page, write three 2- and 3-digit addition problems that each have the sum of 872.

Quilt Math: Grades 4–6 Scholastic Teaching Resources

Name _____

Rhode Island

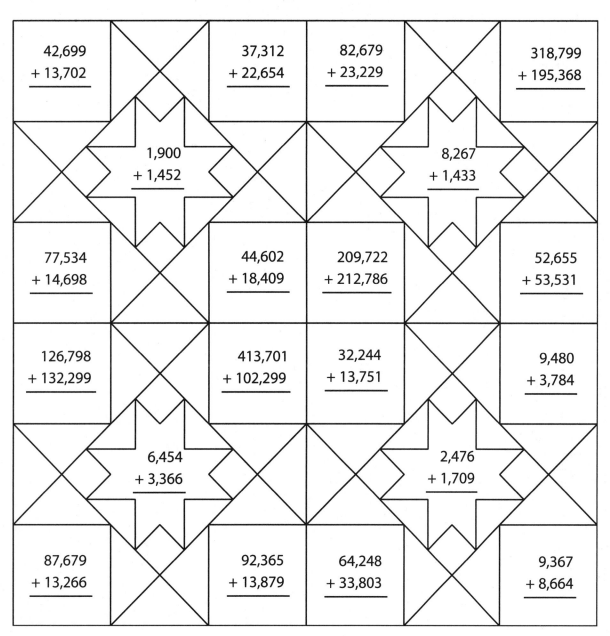

| 42,699
+ 13,702 | | 37,312
+ 22,654 | 82,679
+ 23,229 | | 318,799
+ 195,368 |

| | 1,900
+ 1,452 | | | 8,267
+ 1,433 | |

| 77,534
+ 14,698 | | 44,602
+ 18,409 | 209,722
+ 212,786 | | 52,655
+ 53,531 |

| 126,798
+ 132,299 | | 413,701
+ 102,299 | 32,244
+ 13,751 | | 9,480
+ 3,784 |

| | 6,454
+ 3,366 | | | 2,476
+ 1,709 | |

| 87,679
+ 13,266 | | 92,365
+ 13,879 | 64,248
+ 33,803 | | 9,367
+ 8,664 |

Solve the problems.

If the sum is between	Color the shape
1 and 10,000	red
10,001 and 100,000	blue
100,001 and 1,000,000	yellow

Fill in the other
shapes with
colors of your
choice.

 Extra! • What number when added to 4978 gives the sum of 6000? Write your answer
on the back of this page.

Name_____

Dutch Mill

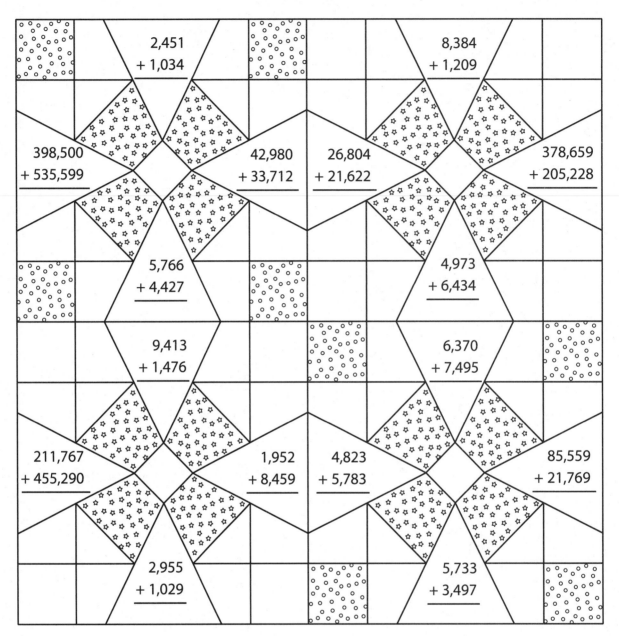

Within the quilt grid:

- 2,451 + 1,034
- 8,384 + 1,209
- 398,500 + 535,599
- 42,980 + 33,712
- 26,804 + 21,622
- 378,659 + 205,228
- 5,766 + 4,427
- 4,973 + 6,434
- 9,413 + 1,476
- 6,370 + 7,495
- 211,767 + 455,290
- 1,952 + 8,459
- 4,823 + 5,783
- 85,559 + 21,769
- 2,955 + 1,029
- 5,733 + 3,497

Solve the problems.

If the sum is between	Color the shape
1 and 10,000	pink
10,001 and 100,000	purple
100,001 and 1,000,000	black

Fill in the other shapes with colors of your choice.

 Extra! On the back of this page, write a five-digit addition problem and sum that has all even digits in the sum.

28

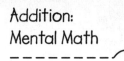

Name _____

Her Sparkling Jewels

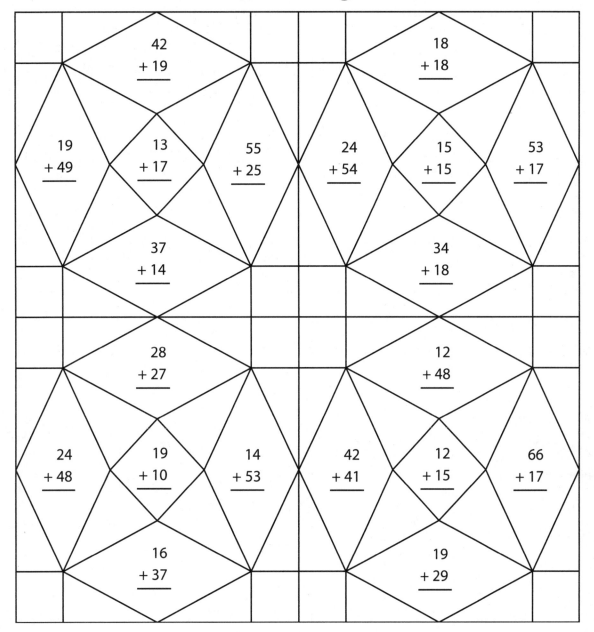

On each line below, write the name of a color that you like.
Then use mental math to find each sum.

If the sum is between	Color the shape
1 and 33	_____
34 and 66	_____
67 and 100	_____

Fill in the other shapes with colors of your choice.

Extra! On the back of this page, write five different addition problems that each have a sum of 10.

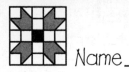

Name _____

Evening Star

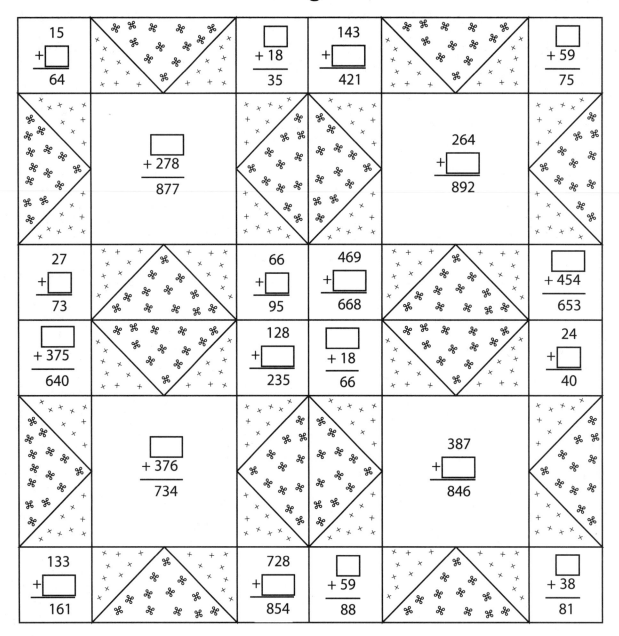

Find the missing addend.

If the addend is between	Color the shape
1 and 50	blue
51 and 300	purple
301 and 1000	red

Fill in the other shapes with colors of your choice.

Extra! On the back of this page, write a three-digit addition problem that has a missing addend, like the problems shown on this page.

30

V-Block

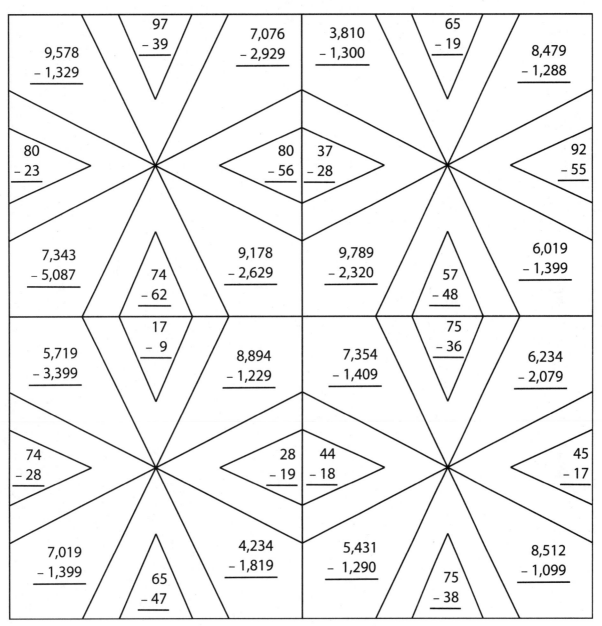

| 9,578
− 1,329 | 97
− 39 | 7,076
− 2,929 | 3,810
− 1,300 | 65
− 19 | 8,479
− 1,288 |

80
− 23   80
− 56   37
− 28   92
− 55

7,343
− 5,087   74
− 62   9,178
− 2,629   9,789
− 2,320   57
− 48   6,019
− 1,399

17
− 9   75
− 36

5,719
− 3,399   8,894
− 1,229   7,354
− 1,409   6,234
− 2,079

74
− 28   28
− 19   44
− 18   45
− 17

7,019
− 1,399   65
− 47   4,234
− 1,819   5,431
− 1,290   75
− 38   8,512
− 1,099

Round each number to the greatest place value.
Then estimate the difference.

If the difference is between	Color the shape
0 and 2,000	yellow
2,010 and 5,000	orange
5,010 and 9,000	dark blue

Fill in the other
shapes with
colors of your
choice.

Extra! On the back of this page, write a subtraction problem that has an estimated
difference of 500.

Name _____

Arkansas Star

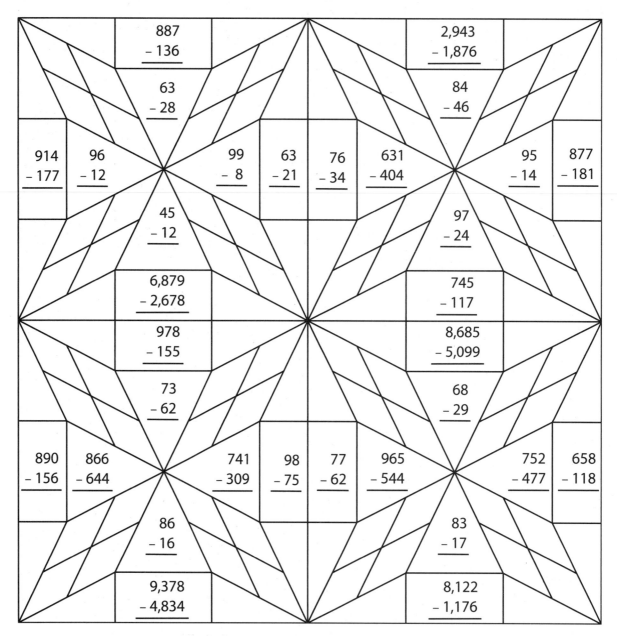

On each line below, write the name of a color that you like. Next, round each number to the greatest place value. Then estimate the difference.

If the difference is between	Color the shape
1 and 80	_____
90 and 500	_____
510 and 10,000	_____

Fill in the other shapes with colors of your choice.

Extra! On the back of this page, write a subtraction problem that has an estimated difference of 800 using the following digits: 1, 2, 5, 7, 8, 9.

32

Name_____

Dove in a Window

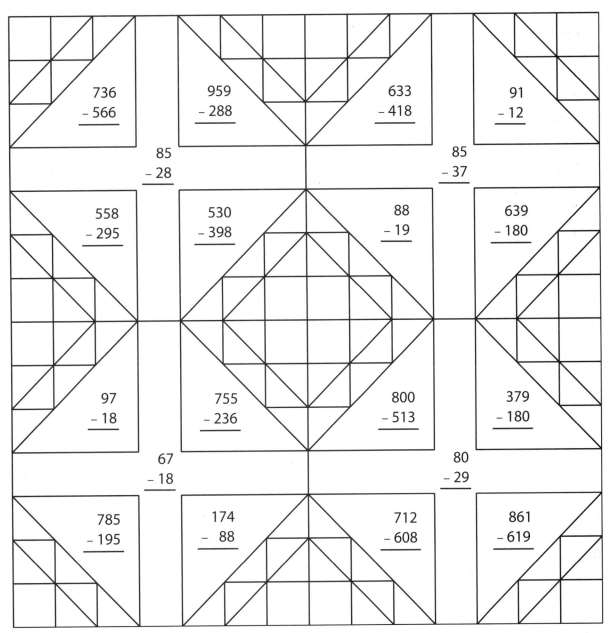

Within the quilt, the following problems appear:

736 − 566

959 − 288

633 − 418

91 − 12

85 − 28

85 − 37

558 − 295

530 − 398

88 − 19

639 − 180

97 − 18

755 − 236

800 − 513

379 − 180

67 − 18

80 − 29

785 − 195

174 − 88

712 − 608

861 − 619

Solve the problems.

If the difference is between	Color the shape
0 and 60	dark pink
61 and 200	purple
201 and 1,000	yellow

Fill in the other shapes with colors of your choice.

Extra! Lisa has 65 candles to sell. If she sells 28 at a craft show and 11 to neighbors, how many candles will she have left? Write your answer on the back of this page.

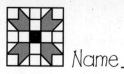

Name_____

Ohio Star

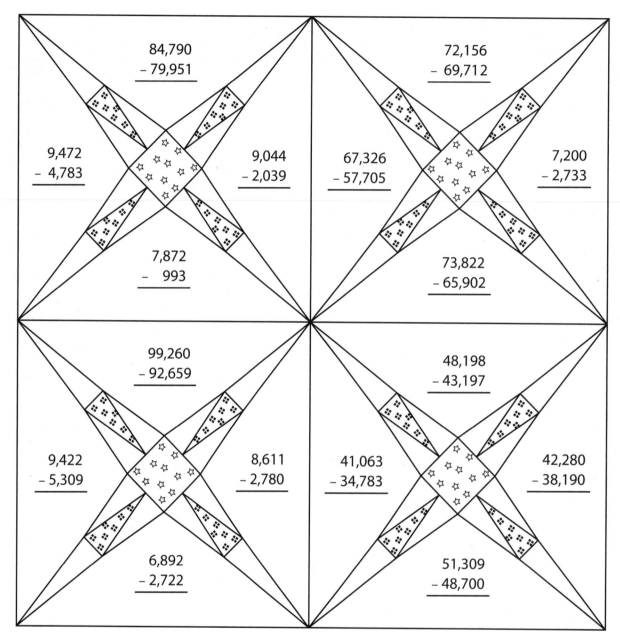

84,790
− 79,951

72,156
− 69,712

9,472
− 4,783

9,044
− 2,039

67,326
− 57,705

7,200
− 2,733

7,872
− 993

73,822
− 65,902

99,260
− 92,659

48,198
− 43,197

9,422
− 5,309

8,611
− 2,780

41,063
− 34,783

42,280
− 38,190

6,892
− 2,722

51,309
− 48,700

On each line below, write the name of a color that you like.
Then find the difference.

If the difference is between	Color the shape
1 and 5,000	_____
5,001 and 10,000	_____

Fill in the other shapes with colors of your choice.

Extra! On the back of this page, create two 4-digit numbers that have the largest possible difference using the following digits: 4, 8, 3, 1, 6, 5, 1, 6.

Name _____

Navajo

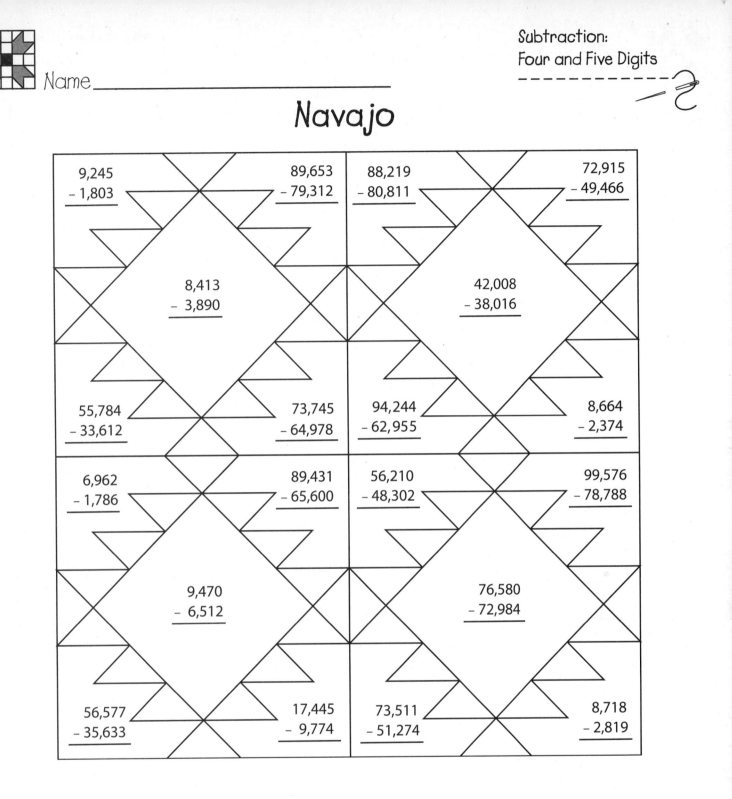

$$9,245 - 1,803$$

$$89,653 - 79,312$$

$$88,219 - 80,811$$

$$72,915 - 49,466$$

$$8,413 - 3,890$$

$$42,008 - 38,016$$

$$55,784 - 33,612$$

$$73,745 - 64,978$$

$$94,244 - 62,955$$

$$8,664 - 2,374$$

$$6,962 - 1,786$$

$$89,431 - 65,600$$

$$56,210 - 48,302$$

$$99,576 - 78,788$$

$$9,470 - 6,512$$

$$76,580 - 72,984$$

$$56,577 - 35,633$$

$$17,445 - 9,774$$

$$73,511 - 51,274$$

$$8,718 - 2,819$$

Solve the problems.

If the difference is between	Color the shape
0 and 5,000	red
5,001 and 10,000	gray
10,001 and 90,000	black

Fill in the other shapes with colors of your choice.

Extra! In 1983, an Olympic skater started skating. In 2001, she skated in her first Olympics. How many years did she skate before her first Olympics? Write your answer on the back of this page.

Name_____

Autograph

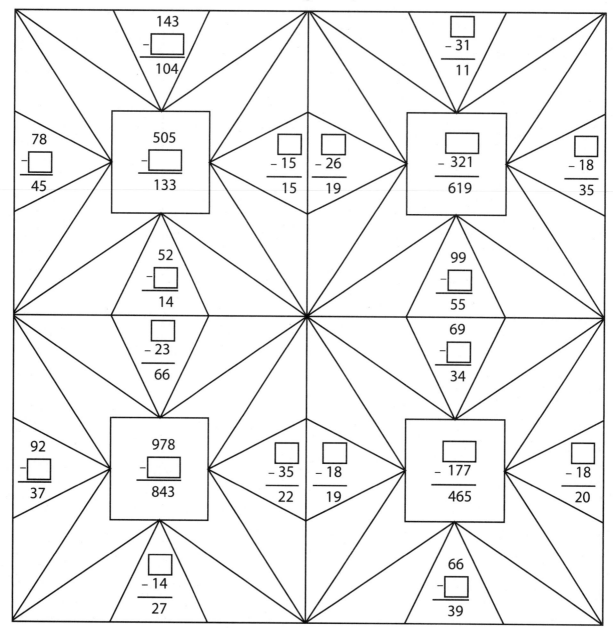

Find each missing number.

If the missing number is between	Color the shape
0 and 40	yellow
41 and 80	orange
81 and 1,000	blue

Fill in the other shapes with colors of your choice.

 Extra! What number when subtracted from 100 equals 33? Write your answer on the back of this page.

Name _____

Broken Dishes

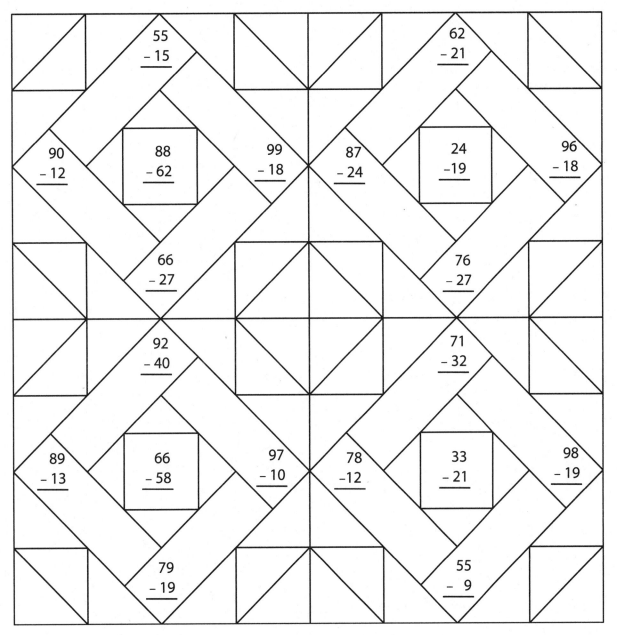

Use mental math to find each difference.

If the difference is between	Color the shape
0 and 30	yellow
31 and 60	red
61 and 100	blue

Fill in the other shapes with colors of your choice.

 Extra! On the back of this page, write three different subtraction problems that can be solved easily using mental math. Have a friend solve your problems.

Colorado

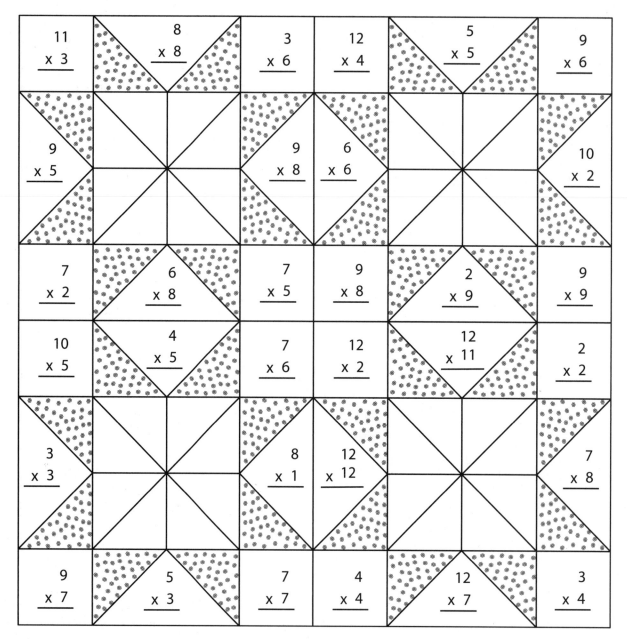

Solve the problems.

If the product is between	Color the shape
1 and 40	yellow
41 and 144	purple

Fill in the other
shapes with
colors of your
choice.

 On the back of this page, write three different multiplication problems that each
have a product of 24.

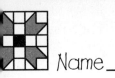

Name_____

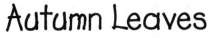

Autumn Leaves

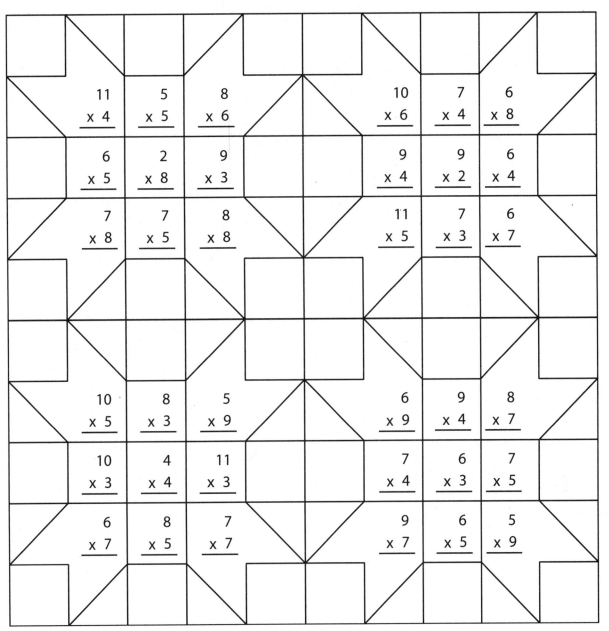

Solve the problems.

If the product is between	Color the shape
0 and 20	yellow
21 and 40	light orange
41 and 65	orange

Fill in the other shapes with colors of your choice.

Extra! • On the back of this page, write two different multiplication problems that each have the same product.

Name_____

Dakota Gold

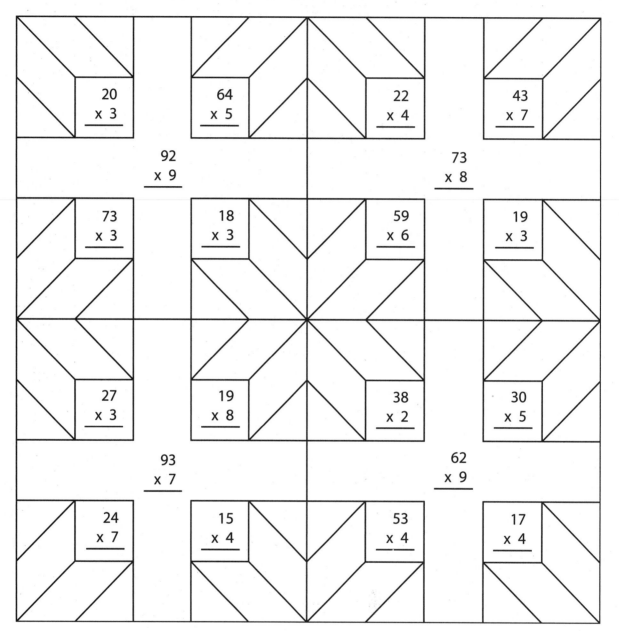

20
x 3

64
x 5

22
x 4

43
x 7

92
x 9

73
x 8

73
x 3

18
x 3

59
x 6

19
x 3

27
x 3

19
x 8

38
x 2

30
x 5

93
x 7

62
x 9

24
x 7

15
x 4

53
x 4

17
x 4

Solve the problems.

If the product is between	Color the shape
0 and 100	red
101 and 400	blue
401 and 1,000	yellow

Fill in the other shapes with colors of your choice.

Extra! On the back of this page, write a multiplication problem that has an even three-digit product.

Name _____

Lucinda's Star

66 x 3		22 x 6	73 x 3		64 x 3
80 x 9	73 x 6			92 x 9	67 x 6
63 x 5	68 x 9		38 x 9		76 x 8
81 x 8	34 x 9		83 x 8		57 x 7
82 x 4	78 x 8			68 x 7	84 x 8
35 x 3		46 x 3	79 x 2		29 x 9
25 x 9		12 x 6	77 x 2		88 x 2
89 x 9	89 x 6			95 x 9	59 x 9
70 x 6	91 x 7		66 x 8		99 x 9
94 x 7	98 x 4		86 x 7		50 x 9
49 x 9	90 x 8			63 x 8	76 x 8
30 x 7		37 x 5	41 x 7		12 x 4

Solve the problems.

If the product is between	Color the shape
0 and 300	green
301 and 600	purple
601 and 1,000	pink

Fill in the other shapes with colors of your choice.

Extra! Find the missing number: 19 x _____ = 95

41

Name_____

Weathervane

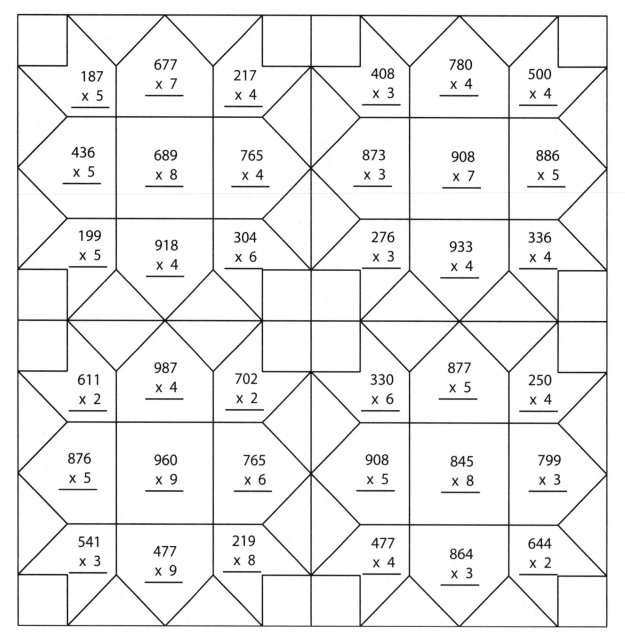

187×5 677×7 217×4 408×3 780×4 500×4

436×5 689×8 765×4 873×3 908×7 886×5

199×5 918×4 304×6 276×3 933×4 336×4

611×2 987×4 702×2 330×6 877×5 250×4

876×5 960×9 765×6 908×5 845×8 799×3

541×3 477×9 219×8 477×4 864×3 644×2

Solve the problems.

If the product is between	Color the shape
1 and 2,000	red
2,001 and 5,000	gray
5,001 and 10,000	black

Fill in the other shapes with colors of your choice.

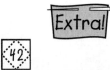 **Extra!** If there are 365 days in one year, how many days are in eight years? Write your answer on the back of this page.

42

Name_____

Windmills and Stars

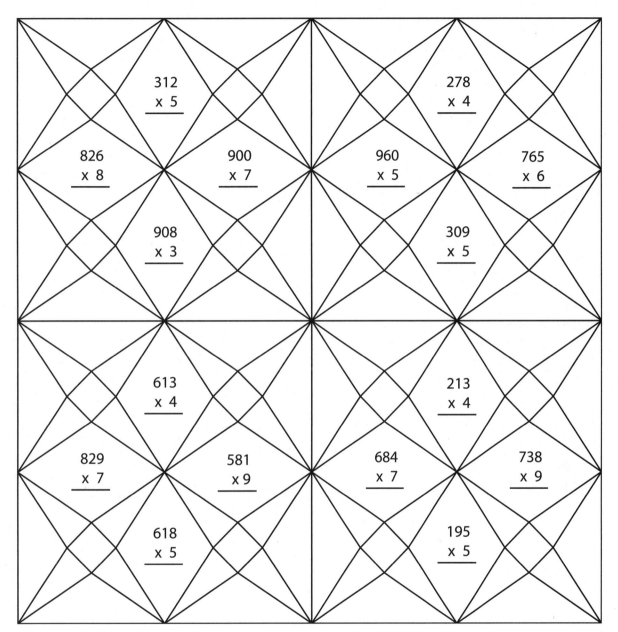

312
x 5

278
x 4

826
x 8

900
x 7

960
x 5

765
x 6

908
x 3

309
x 5

613
x 4

213
x 4

829
x 7

581
x 9

684
x 7

738
x 9

618
x 5

195
x 5

Solve the problems.

If the product is between	Color the shape
0 and 4,500	light purple
4,501 and 10,000	orange

Fill in the other shapes with colors of your choice.

Extra! On the back of this page, write a multiplication problem that has 8 as a factor and a product of 3,288.

Name _____

Maltese Cross

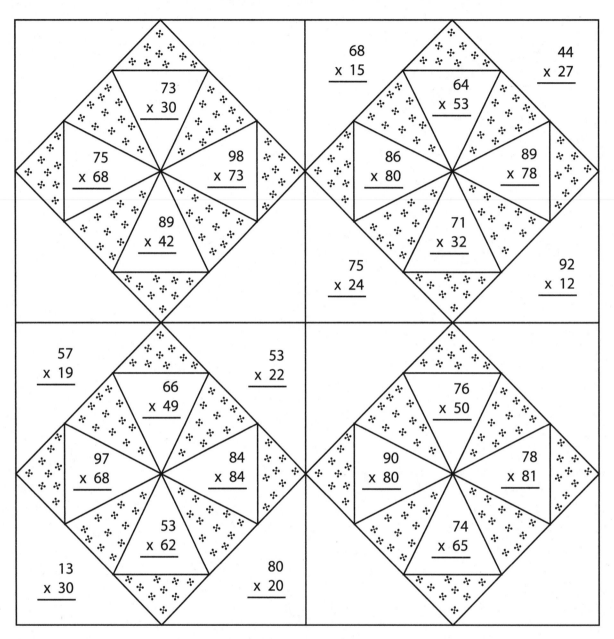

73
x 30

75
x 68

98
x 73

89
x 42

68
x 15

44
x 27

64
x 53

86
x 80

89
x 78

71
x 32

75
x 24

92
x 12

57
x 19

53
x 22

66
x 49

97
x 68

84
x 84

53
x 62

13
x 30

80
x 20

76
x 50

90
x 80

78
x 81

74
x 65

On each line below, write the name of a color that you like.
Then find each product.

If the product is between	Color the shape
1 and 2,000	_____
2,001 and 5,000	_____
5,001 and 10,000	_____

Fill in the other shapes with colors of your choice.

 Extra! On the back of this page, write your age. Then write how old you will be when you are ten times older.

44

Name_____

Flyfoot

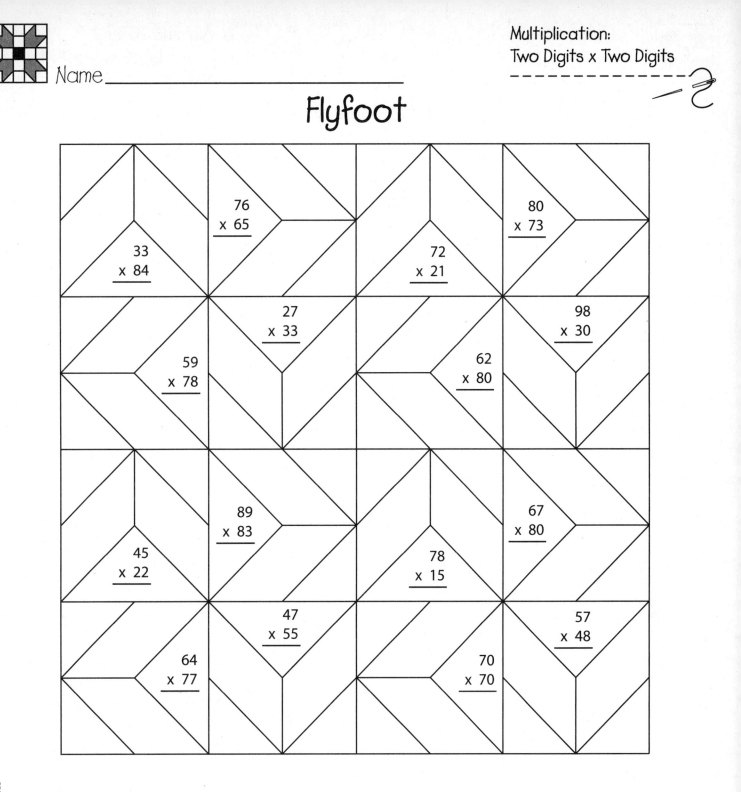

Quilt Math: Grades 4–6 Scholastic Teaching Resources

Solve the problems.

If the product is between	Color the shape
0 and 4,000	blue
4001 and 10,000	yellow

Fill in the other shapes with colors of your choice.

 Extra! ● On the back of this page, write two 2-digit numbers. Multiply them to find the product.

45

Name_____

Rail Fence

124 x 17 = _____

512 x 53 = _____

754 x 99 = _____

987 x 87 = _____

653 x 22 = _____

608 x 67 = _____

832 x 76 = _____

909 x 83 = _____

600 x 14 = _____

768 x 57 = _____

755 x 68 = _____

876 x 92 = _____

509 x 31 = _____

855 x 42 = _____

618 x 94 = _____

900 x 99 = _____

432 x 20 = _____

970 x 34 = _____

627 x 92 = _____

967 x 89 = _____

532 x 39 = _____

477 x 67 = _____

897 x 58 = _____

984 x 90 = _____

655 x 23 = _____

698 x 56 = _____

824 x 77 = _____

798 x 98 = _____

965 x 13 = _____

542 x 68 = _____

961 x 64 = _____

970 x 87 = _____

Solve the problems.

If the product is between	Color the shape
1 and 25,000	yellow
25,001 and 50,000	red
50,001 and 75,000	green
75,001 and 100,000	brown

Fill in the other shapes with colors of your choice. CRAYON

Extra! Find the missing number: _____ x 25 = 3,625

 46

Sparkling Diamond

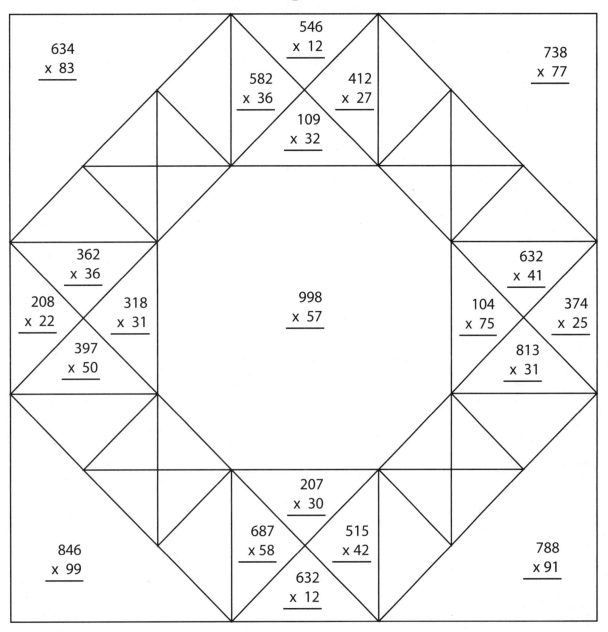

634
x 83

546
x 12

582
x 36

412
x 27

109
x 32

738
x 77

362
x 36

632
x 41

208
x 22

318
x 31

998
x 57

104
x 75

374
x 25

397
x 50

813
x 31

846
x 99

687
x 58

207
x 30

515
x 42

632
x 12

788
x 91

Solve the problems.

If the product is between	Color the shape
1 and 10,000	orange
10,001 and 50,000	green
50,001 and 99,000	blue

Fill in the other shapes with colors of your choice.

Extra! If a multiplication problem has one factor that is 37 and a product of 4625, what is the other factor? Write your answer on the back of this page.

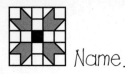

Name _____

Farmer's Daughter

$8\overline{)32}$ $6\overline{)36}$ $3\overline{)9}$ $4\overline{)16}$ $7\overline{)49}$ $6\overline{)18}$

$4\overline{)28}$ $9\overline{)81}$ $8\overline{)56}$ $5\overline{)35}$ $12\overline{)120}$ $4\overline{)32}$

$5\overline{)15}$ $12\overline{)60}$ $6\overline{)12}$ $6\overline{)24}$ $8\overline{)64}$ $11\overline{)33}$

$4\overline{)8}$ $8\overline{)56}$ $9\overline{)18}$ $2\overline{)6}$ $6\overline{)42}$ $12\overline{)48}$

$5\overline{)25}$ $9\overline{)99}$ $6\overline{)42}$ $8\overline{)64}$ $12\overline{)132}$ $12\overline{)72}$

$9\overline{)36}$ $7\overline{)35}$ $11\overline{)22}$ $7\overline{)21}$ $4\overline{)20}$ $4\overline{)12}$

Solve the problems.

If the quotient is between	Color the shape
1 and 4	pink
5 and 8	light purple
9 and 12	dark purple

Fill in the other shapes with colors of your choice.

Extra! On the back of this page, write two different division problems that each have the same quotient.

Quilt Math: Grades 4–6 Scholastic Teaching Resources

Salt Lake City

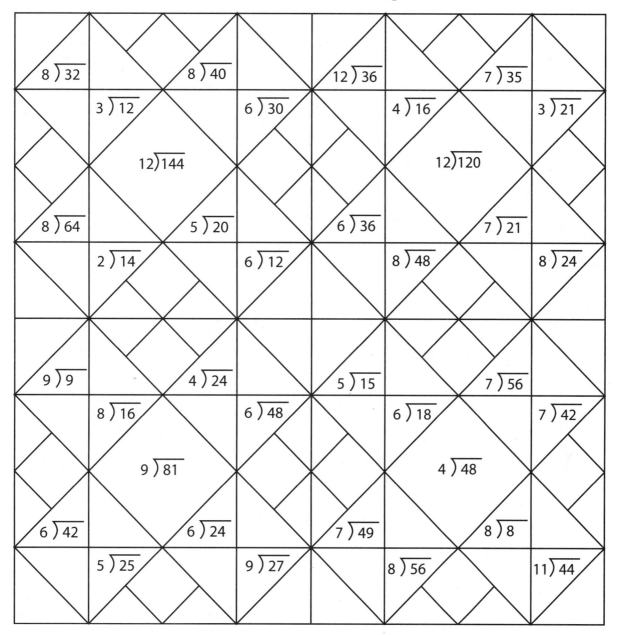

Solve the problems.

If the quotient is between	Color the shape
1 and 4	red
5 and 8	blue
9 and 12	yellow

Fill in the other shapes with colors of your choice.

Extra! On the back of this page, write three different division problems that each have even quotients.

Rolling Star

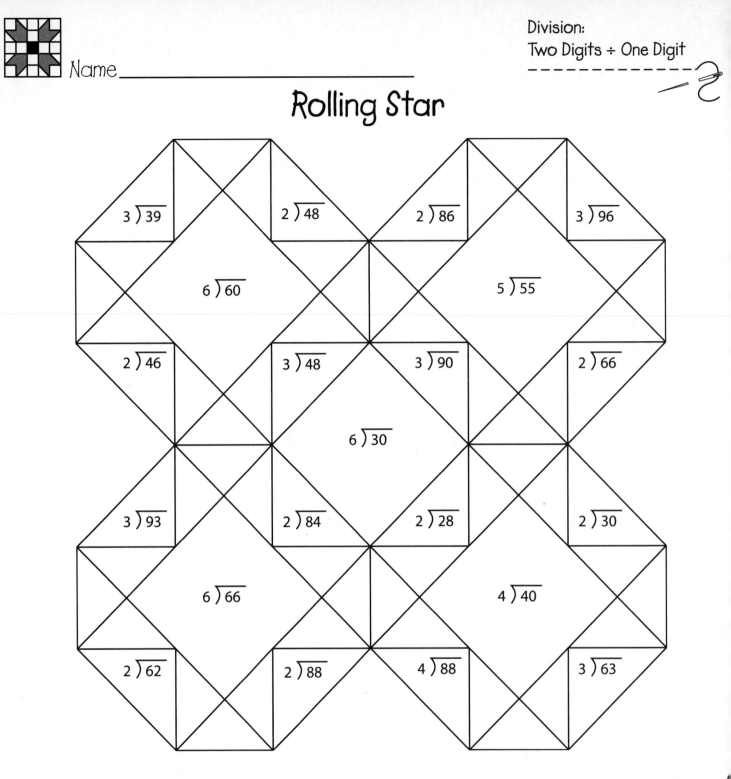

On each line below, write the name of a color that you like.
Then find each quotient.

If the quotient is between	Color the shape
1 and 12	_____
13 and 24	_____
25 and 50	_____

Fill in the other shapes with colors of your choice.

Extra! Identify the missing digit: 4 ___ ÷ 4 = 12

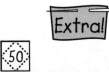

Name _____

Alaska

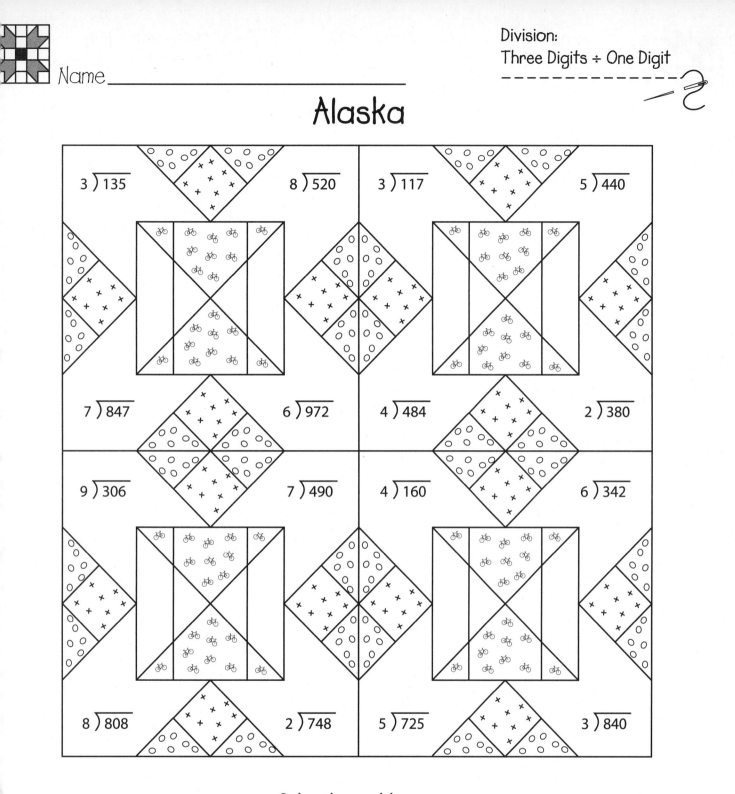

$3\overline{)135}$ $8\overline{)520}$ $3\overline{)117}$ $5\overline{)440}$

$7\overline{)847}$ $6\overline{)972}$ $4\overline{)484}$ $2\overline{)380}$

$9\overline{)306}$ $7\overline{)490}$ $4\overline{)160}$ $6\overline{)342}$

$8\overline{)808}$ $2\overline{)748}$ $5\overline{)725}$ $3\overline{)840}$

Solve the problems.

If the quotient is between	Color the shape
1 and 50	black
51 and 100	pink
101 and 150	purple
151 and 500	blue

Fill in the other shapes with colors of your choice.

Extra! When you divide a three-digit number by a one-digit number, how can you tell, before you divide, if the quotient will have two or three digits? Write your answer on the back of this page.

51

Name _____

Square and a Half

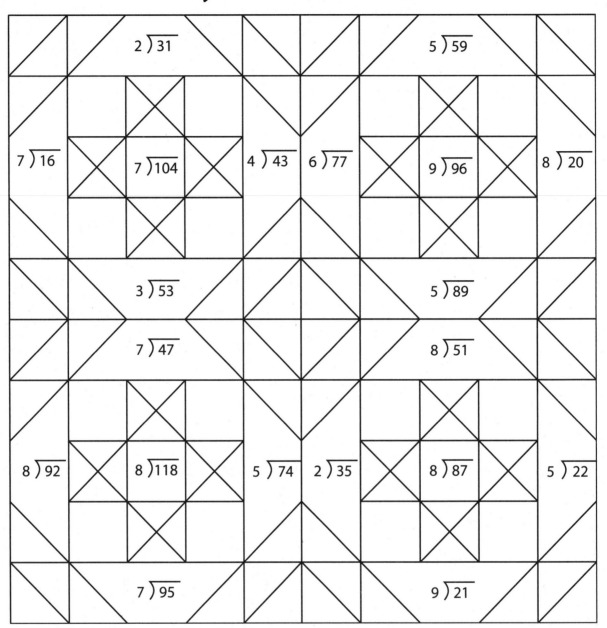

Solve the problems.

If the remainder is between	Color the shape
1 and 3	dark pink
4 and 5	dark purple
6 and 9	yellow

Fill in the other shapes with colors of your choice.

Extra! Create a division problem with the greatest possible remainder using the following digits: 3, 4, 6.

Name_____

Four in Block Work

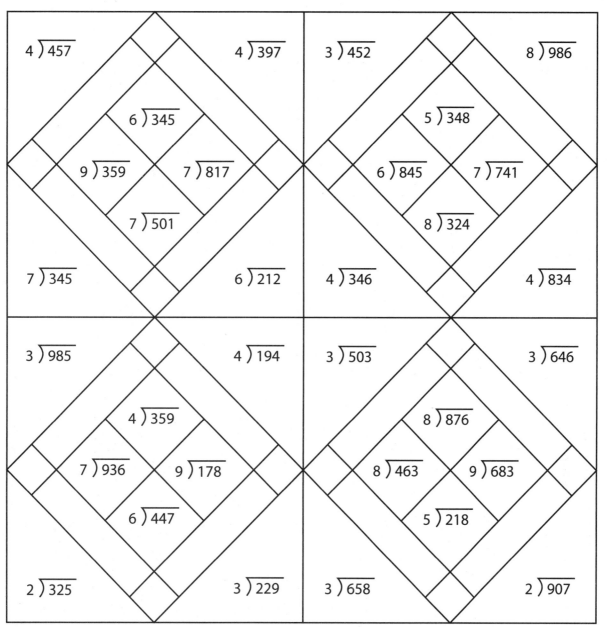

4) 457   4) 397   3) 452   8) 986

6) 345   5) 348

9) 359   7) 817   6) 845   7) 741

7) 501   8) 324

7) 345   6) 212   4) 346   4) 834

3) 985   4) 194   3) 503   3) 646

4) 359   8) 876

7) 936   9) 178   8) 463   9) 683

6) 447   5) 218

2) 325   3) 229   3) 658   2) 907

Solve the problems.

If the remainder is between	Color the shape
0 and 2	light green
3 and 4	pink
5 and 9	yellow

Fill in the other shapes with colors of your choice.

Extra! • If a division problem has a divisor of 9, what is the greatest possible remainder?
Write your answer on the back of this page.

Name_____

All Hallows

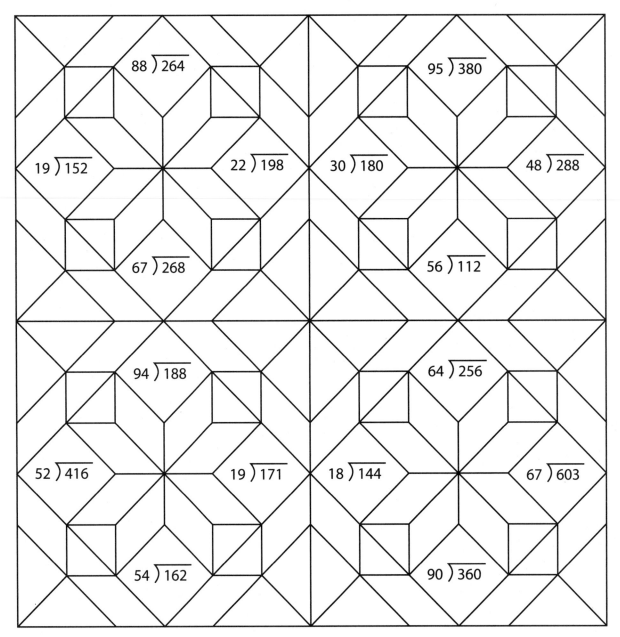

Solve the problems.

If the quotient is between	Color the shape
0 and 4	blue
5 and 9	yellow

Fill in the other shapes with colors of your choice.

Extra! If a division problem has a divisor of 43, what is the greatest possible remainder?
Write your answer on the back of this page.

Name_____

Four Square

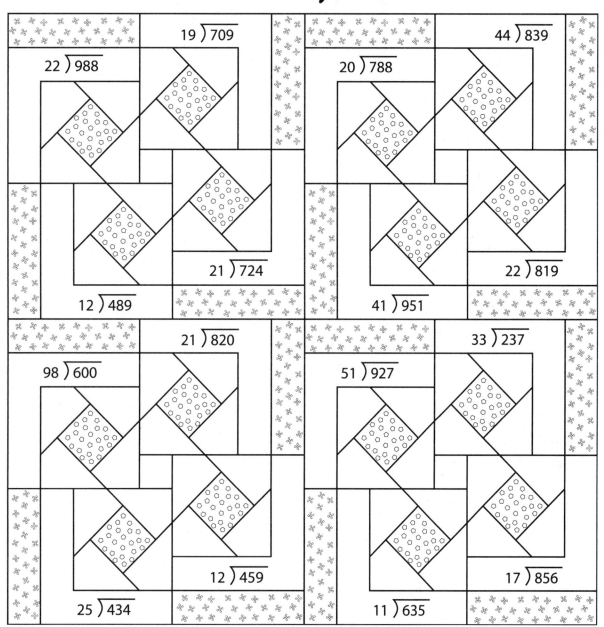

$19\overline{)709}$

$44\overline{)839}$

$22\overline{)988}$

$20\overline{)788}$

$21\overline{)724}$

$22\overline{)819}$

$12\overline{)489}$

$41\overline{)951}$

$21\overline{)820}$

$33\overline{)237}$

$98\overline{)600}$

$51\overline{)927}$

$12\overline{)459}$

$17\overline{)856}$

$25\overline{)434}$

$11\overline{)635}$

Solve the problems.

If the remainder is between	Color the shape
0 and 7	red
8 and 25	black

Fill in the other shapes with colors of your choice.

Extra! When a number is divided by 27, what are the possible remainders? Write your answers on the back of this page.

Name_____

Churn Dash

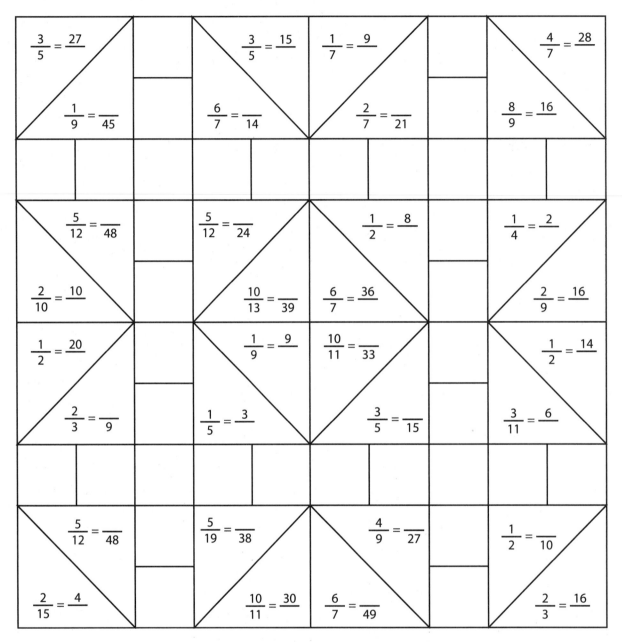

Find the equivalent fractions.

If the answer is between	Color the shape
0 and 10	orange
11 and 22	yellow
23 and 90	blue

Fill in the other shapes with colors of your choice.

Extra! Circle the pairs of equivalent fractions:

$$\frac{4}{5} = \frac{40}{50} \qquad \frac{3}{6} = \frac{1}{3} \qquad \frac{2}{3} = \frac{22}{33} \qquad \frac{1}{12} = \frac{2}{36}$$

Name_____

Louisiana

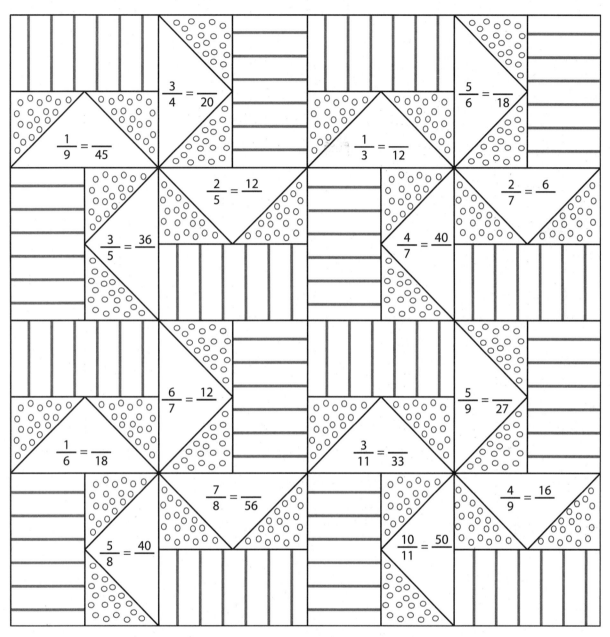

$\frac{3}{4} = \frac{}{20}$

$\frac{5}{6} = \frac{}{18}$

$\frac{1}{9} = \frac{}{45}$

$\frac{1}{3} = \frac{}{12}$

$\frac{2}{5} = \frac{12}{}$

$\frac{2}{7} = \frac{6}{}$

$\frac{3}{5} = \frac{36}{}$

$\frac{4}{7} = \frac{40}{}$

$\frac{6}{7} = \frac{12}{}$

$\frac{5}{9} = \frac{}{27}$

$\frac{1}{6} = \frac{}{18}$

$\frac{3}{11} = \frac{}{33}$

$\frac{7}{8} = \frac{}{56}$

$\frac{4}{9} = \frac{16}{}$

$\frac{5}{8} = \frac{40}{}$

$\frac{10}{11} = \frac{50}{}$

Find the equivalent fractions.

If the answer is between	Color the shape
1 and 10	red
11 and 20	blue
21 and 50	green
51 and 100	yellow

Fill in the other shapes with colors of your choice.

Extra! On the back of this page, write three different fractions that are each equivalent to three-fifths.

Name _____

Mother's Dream

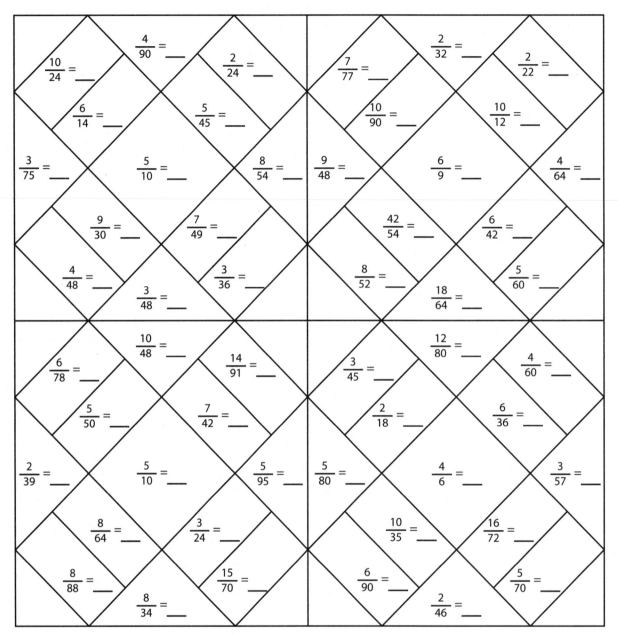

Rename in lowest terms.

If the denominator in the answer is between	Color the shape
0 and 5	yellow
6 and 10	orange
11 and 15	green
16 and 100	blue

Fill in the other shapes with colors of your choice.

Extra! On the back of this page, write three different fractions that are each equivalent to one-half when renamed in lowest terms.

Quilt Math: Grades 4–6 Scholastic Teaching Resources

Name _____

Guiding Star

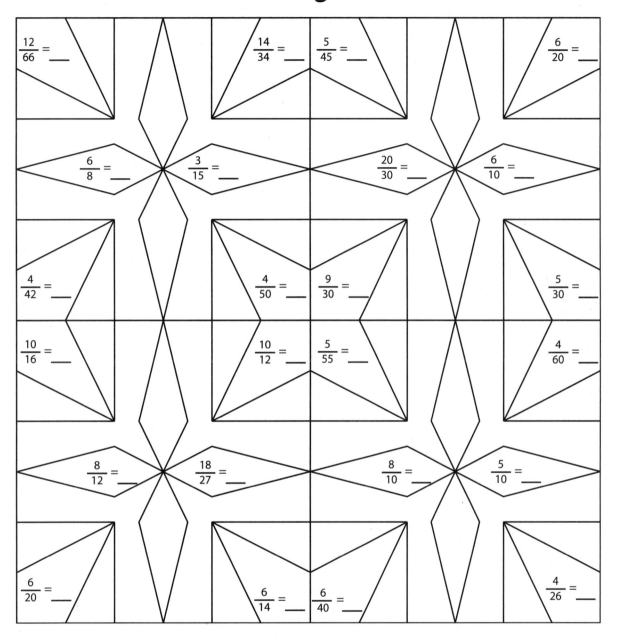

$\frac{12}{66} =$ ___

$\frac{14}{34} =$ ___ $\frac{5}{45} =$ ___

$\frac{6}{20} =$ ___

$\frac{6}{8} =$ ___ $\frac{3}{15} =$ ___

$\frac{20}{30} =$ ___ $\frac{6}{10} =$ ___

$\frac{4}{42} =$ ___

$\frac{4}{50} =$ ___ $\frac{9}{30} =$ ___

$\frac{5}{30} =$ ___

$\frac{10}{16} =$ ___

$\frac{10}{12} =$ ___ $\frac{5}{55} =$ ___

$\frac{4}{60} =$ ___

$\frac{8}{12} =$ ___ $\frac{18}{27} =$ ___

$\frac{8}{10} =$ ___ $\frac{5}{10} =$ ___

$\frac{6}{20} =$ ___

$\frac{6}{14} =$ ___ $\frac{6}{40} =$ ___

$\frac{4}{26} =$ ___

Rename in lowest terms.

If the denominator in the answer is between	Color the shape
0 and 5	yellow
6 and 10	blue
11 and 25	purple

Fill in the other shapes with colors of your choice.

Extra! Circle the fraction that is not equivalent to one-half when renamed in lowest terms:

$\frac{8}{16}$ $\frac{10}{20}$ $\frac{5}{10}$ $\frac{9}{18}$ $\frac{15}{30}$ $\frac{10}{12}$

Name _____

T-Quilt

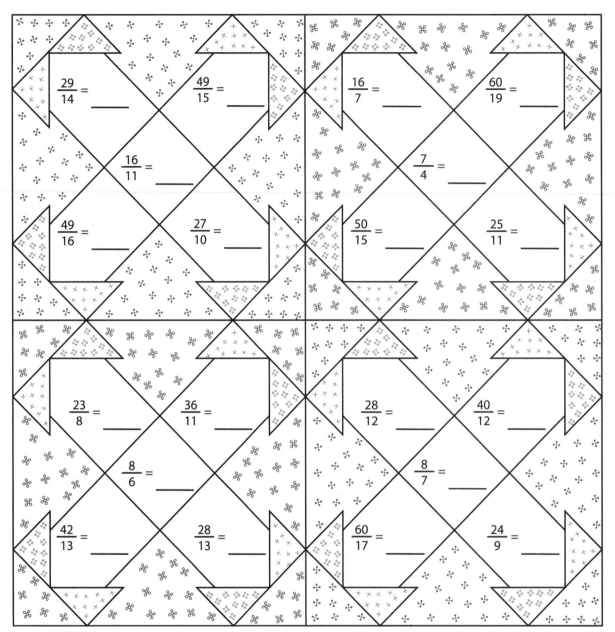

$\frac{29}{14}$ = _____

$\frac{49}{15}$ = _____

$\frac{16}{7}$ = _____

$\frac{60}{19}$ = _____

$\frac{16}{11}$ = _____

$\frac{7}{4}$ = _____

$\frac{49}{16}$ = _____

$\frac{27}{10}$ = _____

$\frac{50}{15}$ = _____

$\frac{25}{11}$ = _____

$\frac{23}{8}$ = _____

$\frac{36}{11}$ = _____

$\frac{28}{12}$ = _____

$\frac{40}{12}$ = _____

$\frac{8}{6}$ = _____

$\frac{8}{7}$ = _____

$\frac{42}{13}$ = _____

$\frac{28}{13}$ = _____

$\frac{60}{17}$ = _____

$\frac{24}{9}$ = _____

On each line below, write the name of a color that you like. Then change
each improper fraction to a mixed number in lowest terms.

If the new number is	Color the shape
greater than 0 but less than 2	_____
greater than 2 but less than 3	_____
greater than 3 but less than 4	_____

Fill in the other
shapes with
colors of your
choice.

 If an improper fraction has 9 as a denominator, what is the largest numerator it could
have and still be less than 3? Write your answer on the back of this page.

Name_____

Lace Handkerchief

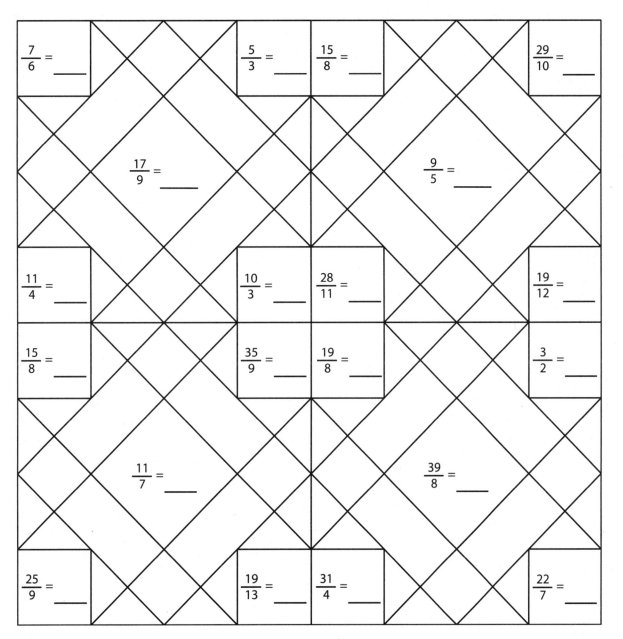

$\frac{7}{6} =$ ____

$\frac{5}{3} =$ ____

$\frac{15}{8} =$ ____

$\frac{29}{10} =$ ____

$\frac{17}{9} =$ ____

$\frac{9}{5} =$ ____

$\frac{11}{4} =$ ____

$\frac{10}{3} =$ ____

$\frac{28}{11} =$ ____

$\frac{19}{12} =$ ____

$\frac{15}{8} =$ ____

$\frac{35}{9} =$ ____

$\frac{19}{8} =$ ____

$\frac{3}{2} =$ ____

$\frac{11}{7} =$ ____

$\frac{39}{8} =$ ____

$\frac{25}{9} =$ ____

$\frac{19}{13} =$ ____

$\frac{31}{4} =$ ____

$\frac{22}{7} =$ ____

Change each improper fraction to a mixed number in lowest terms.

If the numerator in the fraction is between	Color the shape
1 and 5	pink
6 and 10	orange

Fill in the other shapes with colors of your choice.

Extra! ● On the back of this page, write two different improper fractions that are each equivalent to one and one-half.

Name_____

Picture Frames

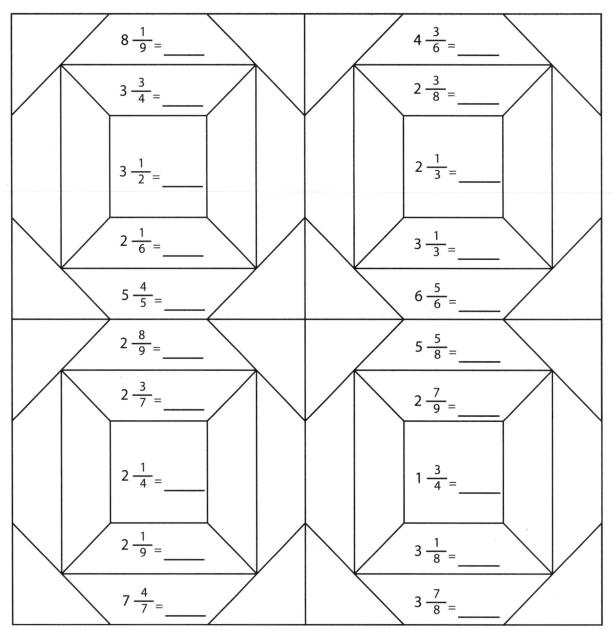

$8\frac{1}{9} =$ _____ $4\frac{3}{6} =$ _____

$3\frac{3}{4} =$ _____ $2\frac{3}{8} =$ _____

$3\frac{1}{2} =$ _____ $2\frac{1}{3} =$ _____

$2\frac{1}{6} =$ _____ $3\frac{1}{3} =$ _____

$5\frac{4}{5} =$ _____ $6\frac{5}{6} =$ _____

$2\frac{8}{9} =$ _____ $5\frac{5}{8} =$ _____

$2\frac{3}{7} =$ _____ $2\frac{7}{9} =$ _____

$2\frac{1}{4} =$ _____ $1\frac{3}{4} =$ _____

$2\frac{1}{9} =$ _____ $3\frac{1}{8} =$ _____

$7\frac{4}{7} =$ _____ $3\frac{7}{8} =$ _____

On each line below, write the name of a color that you like.
Then change each mixed number to an improper fraction.

If the numerator is between	Color the shape
1 and 9	_____
10 and 25	_____
26 and 100	_____

Fill in the other
shapes with
colors of your
choice.

 Extra! ● On the back of this page, write an improper fraction that has a whole number greater
than 5 when changed to a mixed number.

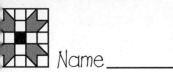

Name_____

Periwinkle

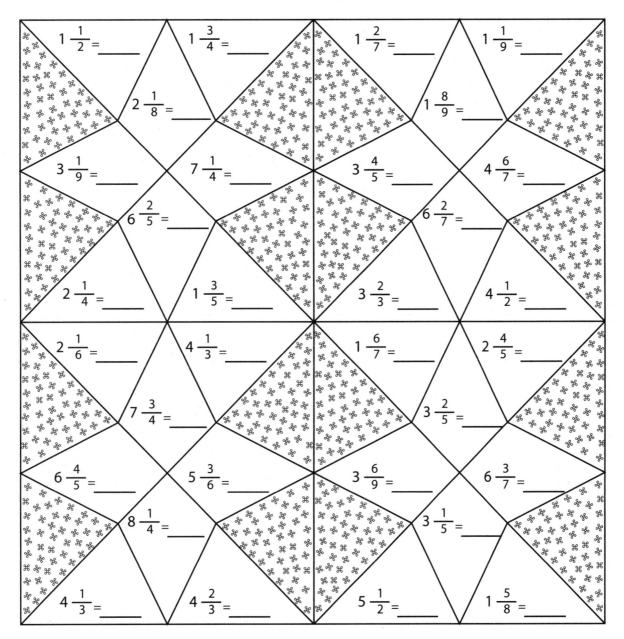

$1\frac{1}{2} =$ _____ $1\frac{3}{4} =$ _____ $1\frac{2}{7} =$ _____ $1\frac{1}{9} =$ _____

$2\frac{1}{8} =$ _____ $1\frac{8}{9} =$ _____

$3\frac{1}{9} =$ _____ $7\frac{1}{4} =$ _____ $3\frac{4}{5} =$ _____ $4\frac{6}{7} =$ _____

$6\frac{2}{5} =$ _____ $6\frac{2}{7} =$ _____

$2\frac{1}{4} =$ _____ $1\frac{3}{5} =$ _____ $3\frac{2}{3} =$ _____ $4\frac{1}{2} =$ _____

$2\frac{1}{6} =$ _____ $4\frac{1}{3} =$ _____ $1\frac{6}{7} =$ _____ $2\frac{4}{5} =$ _____

$7\frac{3}{4} =$ _____ $3\frac{2}{5} =$ _____

$6\frac{4}{5} =$ _____ $5\frac{3}{6} =$ _____ $3\frac{6}{9} =$ _____ $6\frac{3}{7} =$ _____

$8\frac{1}{4} =$ _____ $3\frac{1}{5} =$ _____

$4\frac{1}{3} =$ _____ $4\frac{2}{3} =$ _____ $5\frac{1}{2} =$ _____ $1\frac{5}{8} =$ _____

Change each mixed number to an improper fraction.

If the numerator is between	Color the shape
1 and 15	blue
16 and 45	yellow

Fill in the other
shapes with
colors of your
choice.

Write each mixed number as an improper fraction:

$1\frac{5}{8} =$ _____ $4\frac{2}{3} =$ _____ $6\frac{1}{5} =$ _____

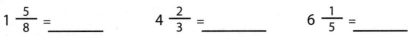

Name_____

Four Pine Trees

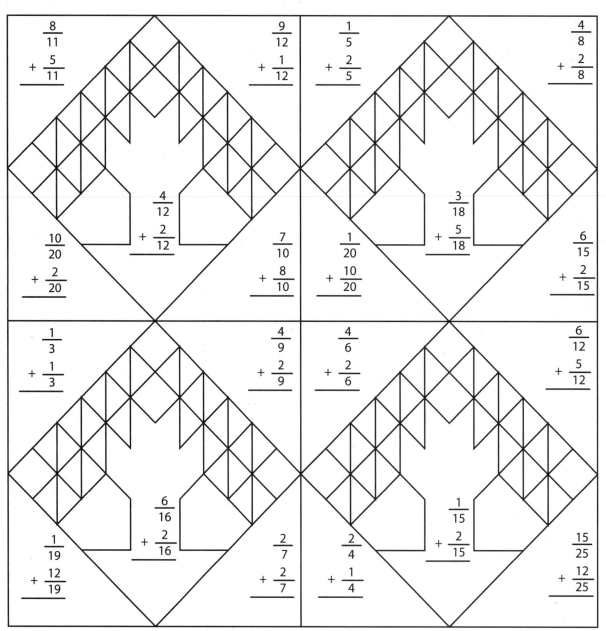

$\frac{8}{11}$
$+\frac{5}{11}$

$\frac{9}{12}$
$+\frac{1}{12}$

$\frac{1}{5}$
$+\frac{2}{5}$

$\frac{4}{8}$
$+\frac{2}{8}$

$\frac{4}{12}$
$+\frac{2}{12}$

$\frac{3}{18}$
$+\frac{5}{18}$

$\frac{10}{20}$
$+\frac{2}{20}$

$\frac{7}{10}$
$+\frac{8}{10}$

$\frac{1}{20}$
$+\frac{10}{20}$

$\frac{6}{15}$
$+\frac{2}{15}$

$\frac{1}{3}$
$+\frac{1}{3}$

$\frac{4}{9}$
$+\frac{2}{9}$

$\frac{4}{6}$
$+\frac{2}{6}$

$\frac{6}{12}$
$+\frac{5}{12}$

$\frac{6}{16}$
$+\frac{2}{16}$

$\frac{1}{15}$
$+\frac{2}{15}$

$\frac{1}{19}$
$+\frac{12}{19}$

$\frac{2}{7}$
$+\frac{2}{7}$

$\frac{2}{4}$
$+\frac{1}{4}$

$\frac{15}{25}$
$+\frac{12}{25}$

Solve the problems. Rename in lowest terms.

If the sum is	Color the shape
$\frac{1}{2}$ or less	orange
greater than $\frac{1}{2}$	brown

Fill in the other
shapes with
colors of your
choice.

  On the back of this page, use fractions to write an addition problem that has
a sum of 1.

Name _____

Oh, Susanna

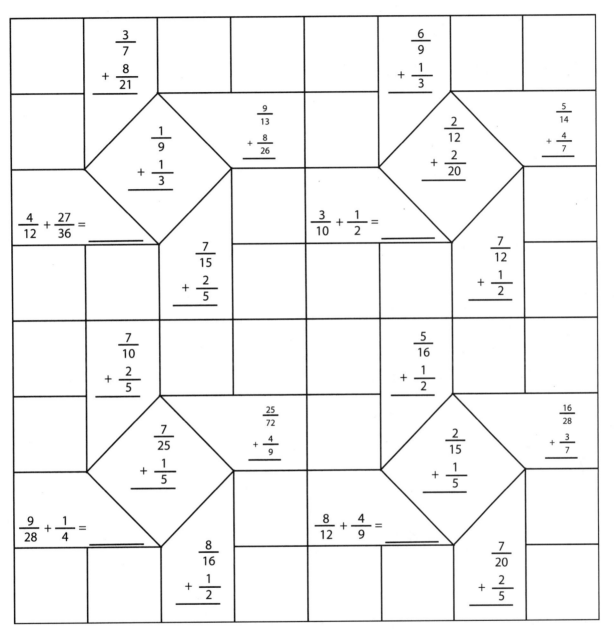

Grid puzzle with the following addition problems:

$\frac{3}{7} + \frac{8}{21}$

$\frac{6}{9} + \frac{1}{3}$

$\frac{1}{9} + \frac{1}{3}$

$\frac{9}{13} + \frac{8}{26}$

$\frac{2}{12} + \frac{2}{20}$

$\frac{5}{14} + \frac{4}{7}$

$\frac{4}{12} + \frac{27}{36} =$ _____

$\frac{3}{10} + \frac{1}{2} =$ _____

$\frac{7}{15} + \frac{2}{5}$

$\frac{7}{12} + \frac{1}{2}$

$\frac{7}{10} + \frac{2}{5}$

$\frac{5}{16} + \frac{1}{2}$

$\frac{7}{25} + \frac{1}{5}$

$\frac{25}{72} + \frac{4}{9}$

$\frac{2}{15} + \frac{1}{5}$

$\frac{16}{28} + \frac{3}{7}$

$\frac{9}{28} + \frac{1}{4} =$ _____

$\frac{8}{12} + \frac{4}{9} =$ _____

$\frac{8}{16} + \frac{1}{2}$

$\frac{7}{20} + \frac{2}{5}$

Solve the problems. Rename in lowest terms.

If the sum is	Color the shape
less than $\frac{1}{2}$	red
greater than $\frac{1}{2}$ but less than 1	gray
1 or greater	black

Fill in the other shapes with colors of your choice. CRAYON

Extra! Find the missing numerator: $\frac{}{12} + \frac{1}{3} = 1$

65

Name_____

Flower Bed

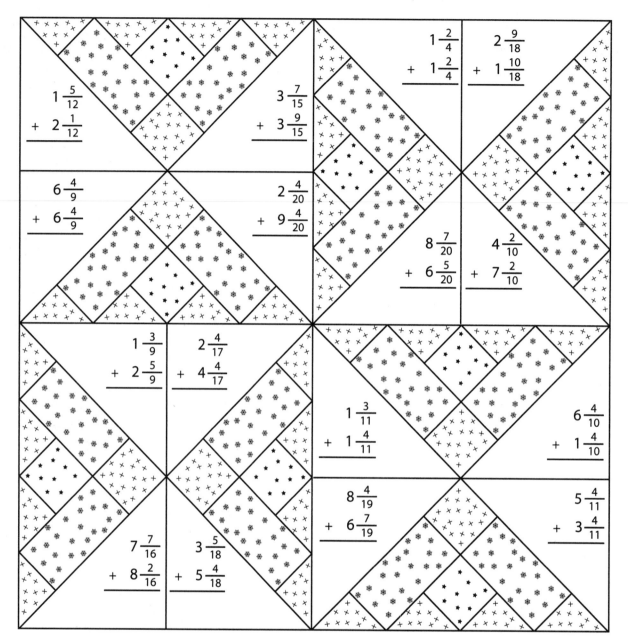

Solve the problems. Rename in lowest terms.

If the sum is	Color the shape
greater than 0 but less than 4	purple
greater than 4 but less than 8	red
greater than 8 but less than 12	yellow
greater than 12 but less than 16	green

Fill in the other
shapes with
colors of your
choice.

Extra! Write the missing numerator: $2\frac{1}{4} + 2\frac{}{16} = 4\frac{3}{4}$

66

Name_____

Lady of the White House

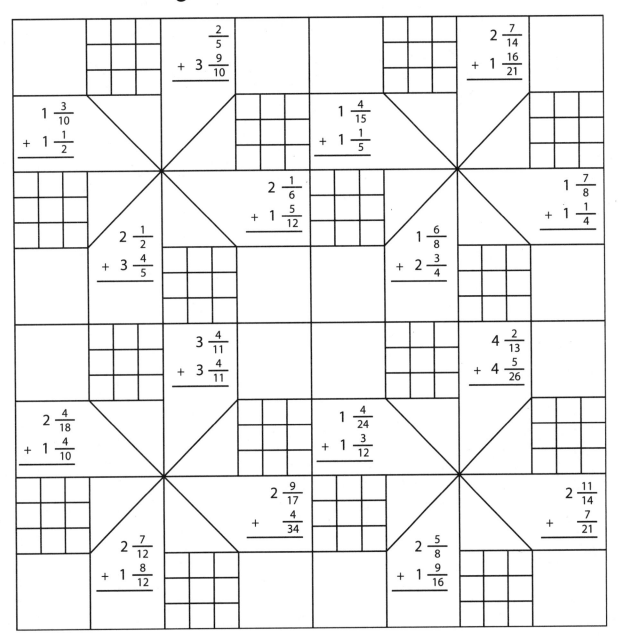

Solve the problems. Rename in lowest terms.

If the sum is	Color the shape
greater than 0 but less than 4	red
greater than 4 but less than 9	blue

Fill in the other shapes with colors of your choice.

Extra! On back of this page, use mixed numbers to write an addition problem that has a sum less than 3.

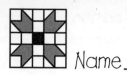

Name_____

Dutch Rose

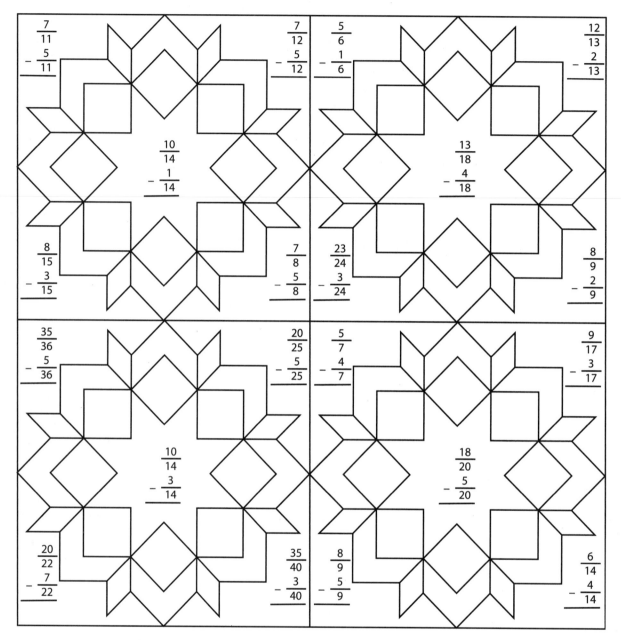

$\frac{7}{11}$ $-\frac{5}{11}$

$\frac{7}{12}$ $-\frac{5}{12}$

$\frac{5}{6}$ $-\frac{1}{6}$

$\frac{12}{13}$ $-\frac{2}{13}$

$\frac{10}{14}$ $-\frac{1}{14}$

$\frac{13}{18}$ $-\frac{4}{18}$

$\frac{8}{15}$ $-\frac{3}{15}$

$\frac{7}{8}$ $-\frac{5}{8}$

$\frac{23}{24}$ $-\frac{3}{24}$

$\frac{8}{9}$ $-\frac{2}{9}$

$\frac{35}{36}$ $-\frac{5}{36}$

$\frac{20}{25}$ $-\frac{5}{25}$

$\frac{5}{7}$ $-\frac{4}{7}$

$\frac{9}{17}$ $-\frac{3}{17}$

$\frac{10}{14}$ $-\frac{3}{14}$

$\frac{18}{20}$ $-\frac{5}{20}$

$\frac{20}{22}$ $-\frac{7}{22}$

$\frac{35}{40}$ $-\frac{3}{40}$

$\frac{8}{9}$ $-\frac{5}{9}$

$\frac{6}{14}$ $-\frac{4}{14}$

Solve the problems. Rename in lowest terms.

If the difference is	Color the shape
$\frac{1}{2}$ or less	pink
greater than $\frac{1}{2}$	green

Fill in the other shapes with colors of your choice.

Extra! On the back of this page, use fractions to write a subtraction problem that has a difference of $\frac{1}{8}$.

Quilt Math: Grades 4–6 Scholastic Teaching Resources

Windstorm

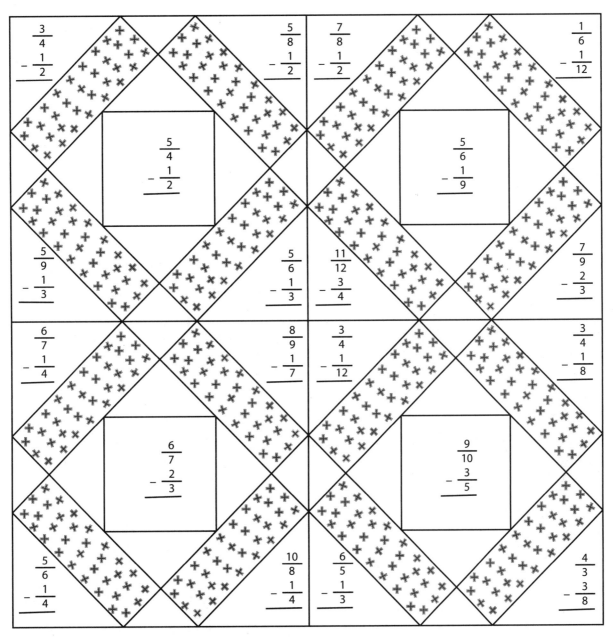

Solve the problems. Rename in lowest terms.

If the difference is	Color the shape
one half or less	red
greater than one half	purple

Fill in the other shapes with colors of your choice.

Extra! On the back of this page, use fractions with unlike denominators to write a subtraction problem that has a difference less than $\frac{1}{2}$.

Name _____

Navajo Squash Blossom

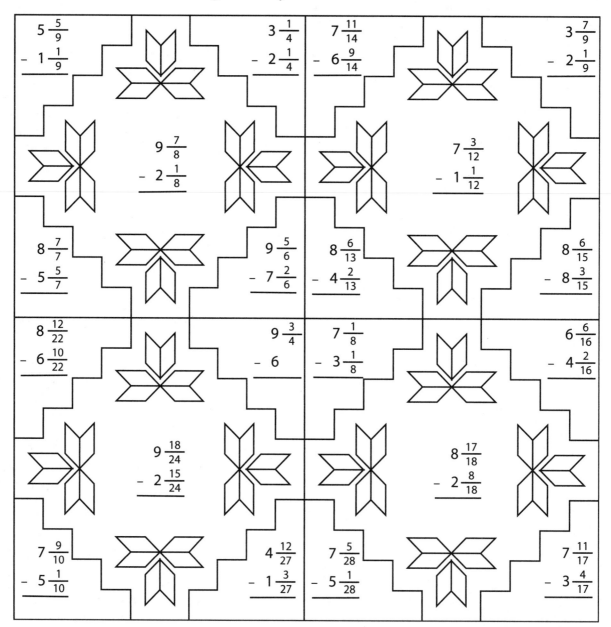

$5\frac{5}{9}$
$- \ 1\frac{1}{9}$

$3\frac{1}{4}$
$- \ 2\frac{1}{4}$

$7\frac{11}{14}$
$- \ 6\frac{9}{14}$

$3\frac{7}{9}$
$- \ 2\frac{1}{9}$

$9\frac{7}{8}$
$- \ 2\frac{1}{8}$

$7\frac{3}{12}$
$- \ 1\frac{1}{12}$

$8\frac{7}{7}$
$- \ 5\frac{5}{7}$

$9\frac{5}{6}$
$- \ 7\frac{2}{6}$

$8\frac{6}{13}$
$- \ 4\frac{2}{13}$

$8\frac{6}{15}$
$- \ 8\frac{3}{15}$

$8\frac{12}{22}$
$- \ 6\frac{10}{22}$

$9\frac{3}{4}$
$- \ 6$

$7\frac{1}{8}$
$- \ 3\frac{1}{8}$

$6\frac{6}{16}$
$- \ 4\frac{2}{16}$

$9\frac{18}{24}$
$- \ 2\frac{15}{24}$

$8\frac{17}{18}$
$- \ 2\frac{8}{18}$

$7\frac{9}{10}$
$- \ 5\frac{1}{10}$

$4\frac{12}{27}$
$- \ 1\frac{3}{27}$

$7\frac{5}{28}$
$- \ 5\frac{1}{28}$

$7\frac{11}{17}$
$- \ 3\frac{4}{17}$

Solve the problems. Rename in lowest terms.

If the difference is	Color the shape
greater than 0 but less than 5	red
greater than 5 but less than 9	green

Fill in the other
shapes with
colors of your
choice.

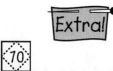 • On the back of this page, use mixed numbers to write a subtraction word problem.
Include the answer, too.

Name _____

Japanese Flower

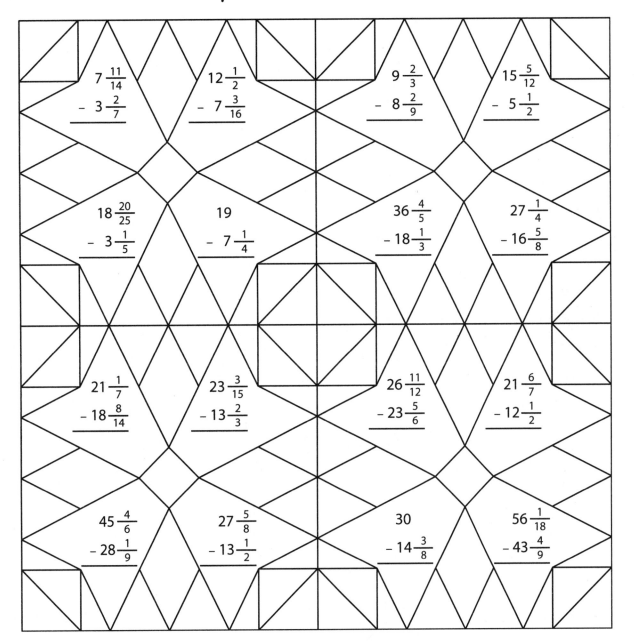

$$7\frac{11}{14}$$
$$-\ 3\frac{2}{7}$$

$$12\frac{1}{2}$$
$$-\ 7\frac{3}{16}$$

$$9\frac{2}{3}$$
$$-\ 8\frac{2}{9}$$

$$15\frac{5}{12}$$
$$-\ 5\frac{1}{2}$$

$$18\frac{20}{25}$$
$$-\ 3\frac{1}{5}$$

$$19$$
$$-\ 7\frac{1}{4}$$

$$36\frac{4}{5}$$
$$-\ 18\frac{1}{3}$$

$$27\frac{1}{4}$$
$$-\ 16\frac{5}{8}$$

$$21\frac{1}{7}$$
$$-\ 18\frac{8}{14}$$

$$23\frac{3}{15}$$
$$-\ 13\frac{2}{3}$$

$$26\frac{11}{12}$$
$$-\ 23\frac{5}{6}$$

$$21\frac{6}{7}$$
$$-\ 12\frac{1}{2}$$

$$45\frac{4}{6}$$
$$-\ 28\frac{1}{9}$$

$$27\frac{5}{8}$$
$$-\ 13\frac{1}{2}$$

$$30$$
$$-\ 14\frac{3}{8}$$

$$56\frac{1}{18}$$
$$-\ 43\frac{4}{9}$$

Solve the problems. Rename in lowest terms.

If the difference is	Color the shape
greater than 0 but less than 5	blue
greater than 5 but less than 10	purple
greater than 10 but less than 15	red
greater than 15 but less than 20	pink

Fill in the other
shapes with
colors of your
choice.

Extra! On the back of this page, use mixed numbers to write a subtraction problem that has
a difference less than 1.

Name_____

Name _____

Houndstooth

Name _____

Fractions: Whole
Numbers x Fractions

Houndstooth

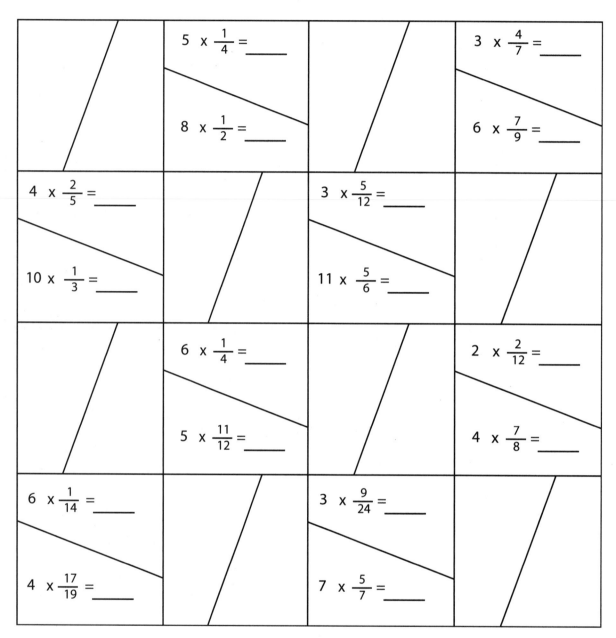

$5 \times \frac{1}{4} =$ _____

$8 \times \frac{1}{2} =$ _____

$3 \times \frac{4}{7} =$ _____

$6 \times \frac{7}{9} =$ _____

$4 \times \frac{2}{5} =$ _____

$10 \times \frac{1}{3} =$ _____

$3 \times \frac{5}{12} =$ _____

$11 \times \frac{5}{6} =$ _____

$6 \times \frac{1}{4} =$ _____

$5 \times \frac{11}{12} =$ _____

$2 \times \frac{2}{12} =$ _____

$4 \times \frac{7}{8} =$ _____

$6 \times \frac{1}{14} =$ _____

$4 \times \frac{17}{19} =$ _____

$3 \times \frac{9}{24} =$ _____

$7 \times \frac{5}{7} =$ _____

Solve the problems. Rename in lowest terms.

If the product is	Color the shape
greater than 0 but less than 3	purple
greater than 3 but less than 15	red

Fill in the other shapes with colors of your choice.

Extra! Circle the problem that has a product that is not a mixed number:

$7 \times \frac{11}{12} =$ _____ $14 \times \frac{1}{9} =$ _____ $7 \times \frac{3}{7} =$ _____

72

Quilt Math: Grades 4–6 Scholastic Teaching Resources

Name_____

Pine Burr

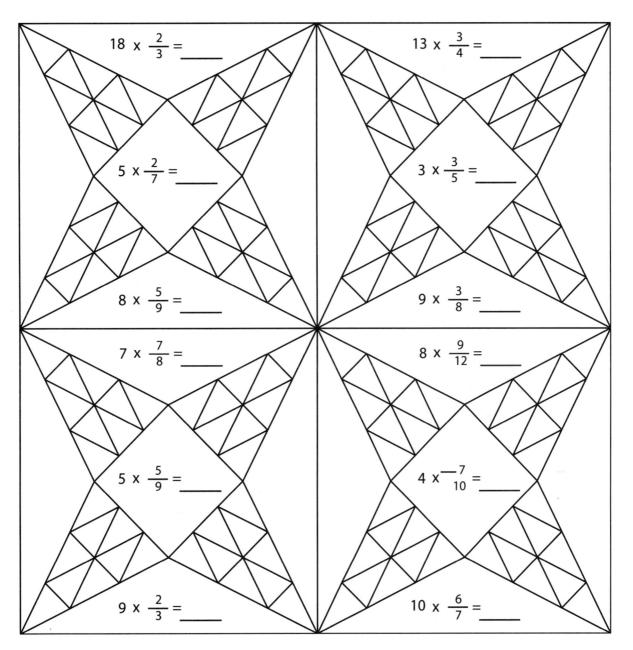

$18 \times \frac{2}{3} =$ _____

$13 \times \frac{3}{4} =$ _____

$5 \times \frac{2}{7} =$ _____

$3 \times \frac{3}{5} =$ _____

$8 \times \frac{5}{9} =$ _____

$9 \times \frac{3}{8} =$ _____

$7 \times \frac{7}{8} =$ _____

$8 \times \frac{9}{12} =$ _____

$5 \times \frac{5}{9} =$ _____

$4 \times \frac{7}{10} =$ _____

$9 \times \frac{2}{3} =$ _____

$10 \times \frac{6}{7} =$ _____

Solve the problems. Rename in lowest terms.

If the product is	Color the shape
greater than 0 but less than 3	yellow
greater than 3 but less than 15	green

Fill in the other shapes with colors of your choice.

Extra! Find the missing numbers:

____ $\times \frac{1}{4} = \frac{3}{4}$

____ $\times \frac{1}{5} = \frac{4}{5}$

____ $\times \frac{1}{10} = \frac{1}{2}$

Name_____

Square in the Center

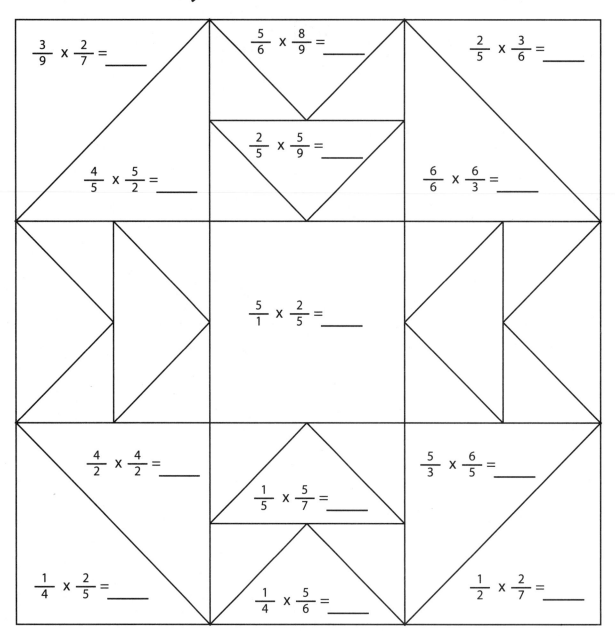

$\frac{3}{9}$ x $\frac{2}{7}$ = _____

$\frac{5}{6}$ x $\frac{8}{9}$ = _____

$\frac{2}{5}$ x $\frac{3}{6}$ = _____

$\frac{2}{5}$ x $\frac{5}{9}$ = _____

$\frac{4}{5}$ x $\frac{5}{2}$ = _____

$\frac{6}{6}$ x $\frac{6}{3}$ = _____

$\frac{5}{1}$ x $\frac{2}{5}$ = _____

$\frac{4}{2}$ x $\frac{4}{2}$ = _____

$\frac{5}{3}$ x $\frac{6}{5}$ = _____

$\frac{1}{5}$ x $\frac{5}{7}$ = _____

$\frac{1}{4}$ x $\frac{2}{5}$ = _____

$\frac{1}{4}$ x $\frac{5}{6}$ = _____

$\frac{1}{2}$ x $\frac{2}{7}$ = _____

Solve the problems. Rename in lowest terms.

If the product is	Color the shape
greater than 0 but less than 1	orange
greater than 1 but less than 5	purple

Fill in the other shapes with colors of your choice.

Extra! Find the missing fraction to make a true multiplication fact: ___ x $\frac{3}{4}$ = $\frac{1}{4}$

Swirling Sea

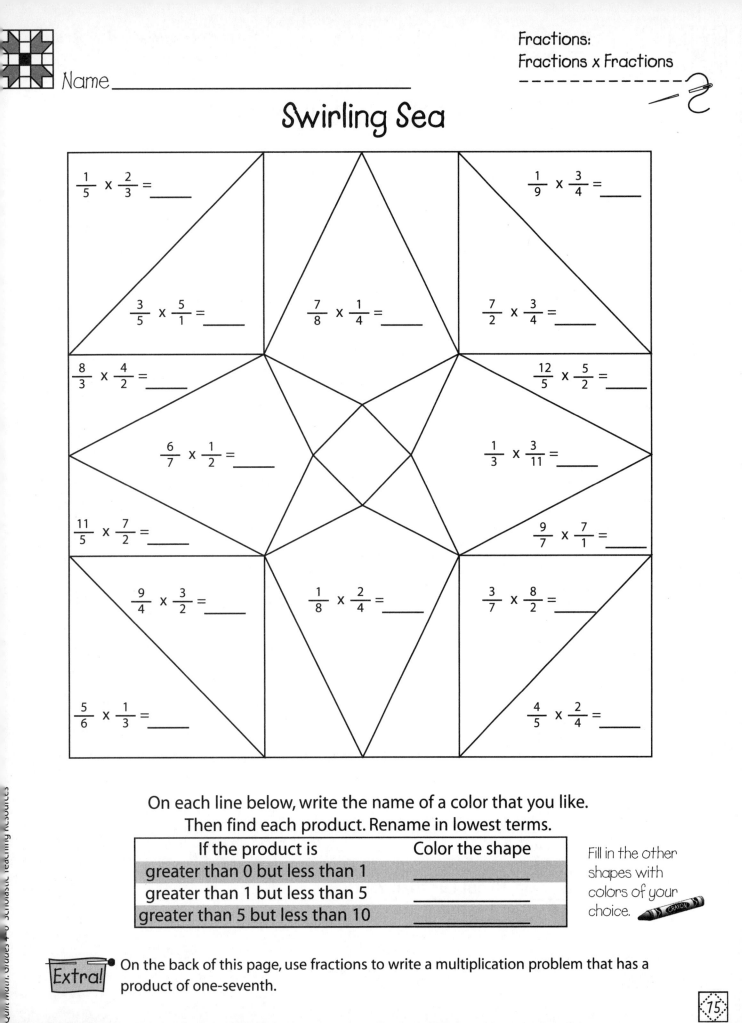

$\frac{1}{5}$ x $\frac{2}{3}$ = _____

$\frac{1}{9}$ x $\frac{3}{4}$ = _____

$\frac{3}{5}$ x $\frac{5}{1}$ = _____

$\frac{7}{8}$ x $\frac{1}{4}$ = _____

$\frac{7}{2}$ x $\frac{3}{4}$ = _____

$\frac{8}{3}$ x $\frac{4}{2}$ = _____

$\frac{12}{5}$ x $\frac{5}{2}$ = _____

$\frac{6}{7}$ x $\frac{1}{2}$ = _____

$\frac{1}{3}$ x $\frac{3}{11}$ = _____

$\frac{11}{5}$ x $\frac{7}{2}$ = _____

$\frac{9}{7}$ x $\frac{7}{1}$ = _____

$\frac{9}{4}$ x $\frac{3}{2}$ = _____

$\frac{1}{8}$ x $\frac{2}{4}$ = _____

$\frac{3}{7}$ x $\frac{8}{2}$ = _____

$\frac{5}{6}$ x $\frac{1}{3}$ = _____

$\frac{4}{5}$ x $\frac{2}{4}$ = _____

On each line below, write the name of a color that you like.
Then find each product. Rename in lowest terms.

If the product is	Color the shape
greater than 0 but less than 1	_____
greater than 1 but less than 5	_____
greater than 5 but less than 10	_____

Fill in the other
shapes with
colors of your
choice.

Extra! On the back of this page, use fractions to write a multiplication problem that has a
product of one-seventh.

Name _____

Next Door Neighbor

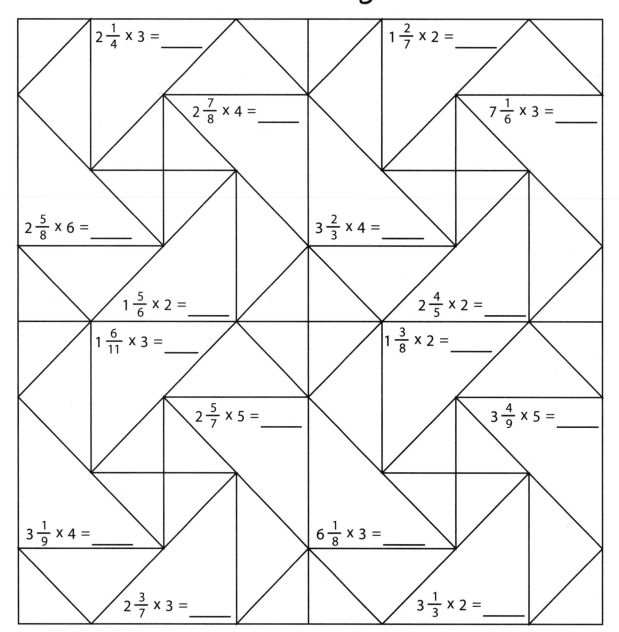

$2\frac{1}{4}$ x 3 = _____

$1\frac{2}{7}$ x 2 = _____

$2\frac{7}{8}$ x 4 = _____

$7\frac{1}{6}$ x 3 = _____

$2\frac{5}{8}$ x 6 = _____

$3\frac{2}{3}$ x 4 = _____

$1\frac{5}{6}$ x 2 = _____

$2\frac{4}{5}$ x 2 = _____

$1\frac{6}{11}$ x 3 = _____

$1\frac{3}{8}$ x 2 = _____

$2\frac{5}{7}$ x 5 = _____

$3\frac{4}{9}$ x 5 = _____

$3\frac{1}{9}$ x 4 = _____

$6\frac{1}{8}$ x 3 = _____

$2\frac{3}{7}$ x 3 = _____

$3\frac{1}{3}$ x 2 = _____

Solve the problems. Rename in lowest terms.

If the product is	Color the shape
greater than 0 but less than 10	orange
greater than 10 but less than 25	black

Fill in the other shapes with colors of your choice.

Extra! Find the missing number: $3\frac{7}{12}$ x _____ = $14\frac{1}{3}$

Name_____

Oklahoma Road

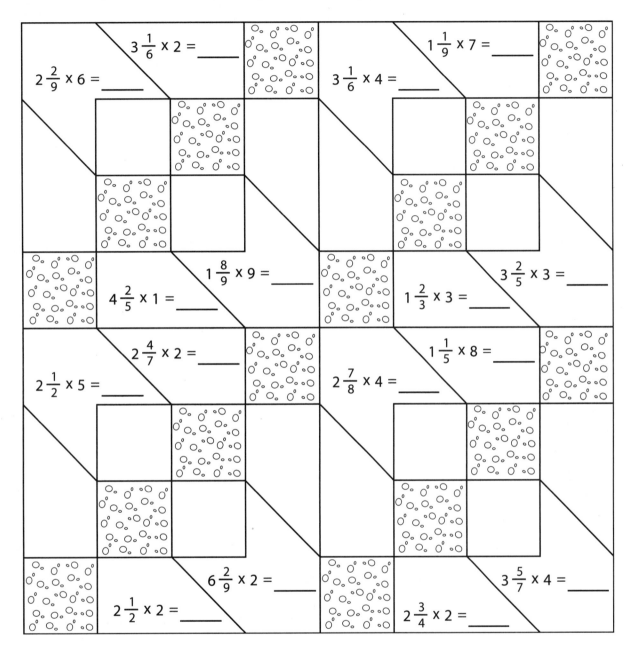

$3\frac{1}{6} \times 2 =$ _____

$2\frac{2}{9} \times 6 =$ _____

$1\frac{1}{9} \times 7 =$ _____

$3\frac{1}{6} \times 4 =$ _____

$1\frac{8}{9} \times 9 =$ _____

$4\frac{2}{5} \times 1 =$ _____

$1\frac{2}{3} \times 3 =$ _____

$3\frac{2}{5} \times 3 =$ _____

$2\frac{4}{7} \times 2 =$ _____

$2\frac{1}{2} \times 5 =$ _____

$1\frac{1}{5} \times 8 =$ _____

$2\frac{7}{8} \times 4 =$ _____

$6\frac{2}{9} \times 2 =$ _____

$2\frac{1}{2} \times 2 =$ _____

$3\frac{5}{7} \times 4 =$ _____

$2\frac{3}{4} \times 2 =$ _____

Solve the problems. Rename in lowest terms.

If the product is	Color the shape
greater than 0 but less than 10	pink
10 or greater	gray

Fill in the other shapes with colors of your choice. 🖍 CRAYON

Extra! Find the missing denominator: $6\frac{1}{\_} \times 2 = 12\frac{1}{4}$

Name _____

Salute to Colors

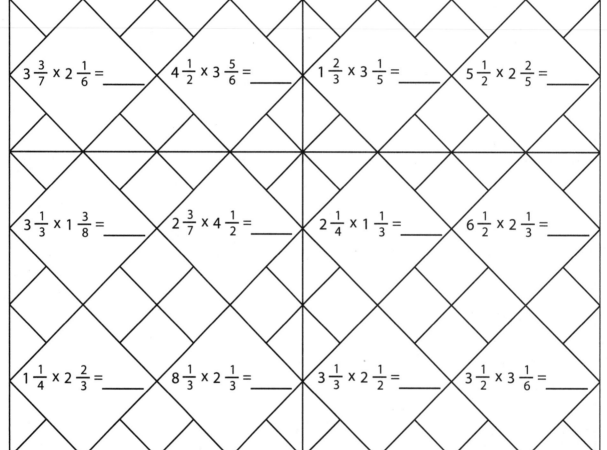

$1\frac{1}{3} \times 2\frac{2}{5} =$ _____ $6\frac{2}{3} \times 4\frac{2}{7} =$ _____ $3\frac{7}{8} \times 1\frac{1}{2} =$ _____ $2\frac{1}{6} \times 7\frac{1}{3} =$ _____

$3\frac{3}{7} \times 2\frac{1}{6} =$ _____ $4\frac{1}{2} \times 3\frac{5}{6} =$ _____ $1\frac{2}{3} \times 3\frac{1}{5} =$ _____ $5\frac{1}{2} \times 2\frac{2}{5} =$ _____

$3\frac{1}{3} \times 1\frac{3}{8} =$ _____ $2\frac{3}{7} \times 4\frac{1}{2} =$ _____ $2\frac{1}{4} \times 1\frac{1}{3} =$ _____ $6\frac{1}{2} \times 2\frac{1}{3} =$ _____

$1\frac{1}{4} \times 2\frac{2}{3} =$ _____ $8\frac{1}{3} \times 2\frac{1}{3} =$ _____ $3\frac{1}{3} \times 2\frac{1}{2} =$ _____ $3\frac{1}{2} \times 3\frac{1}{6} =$ _____

Solve the problems. Rename in lowest terms.

If the product is	Color the shape
greater than 0 but less than 10	red
greater than 10	blue

Fill in the other
shapes with
colors of your
choice.

 On the back of this page, use mixed fractions to write a multiplication problem
that has a product less than 3.

Name_____

Starry Night

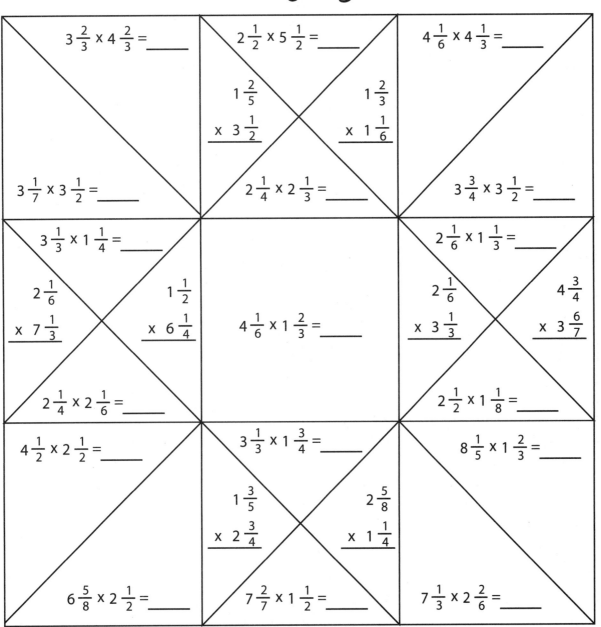

$3\frac{2}{3}$ x $4\frac{2}{3}$ = _____

$2\frac{1}{2}$ x $5\frac{1}{2}$ = _____

$4\frac{1}{6}$ x $4\frac{1}{3}$ = _____

$1\frac{2}{5}$
x $3\frac{1}{2}$

$1\frac{2}{3}$
x $1\frac{1}{6}$

$3\frac{1}{7}$ x $3\frac{1}{2}$ = _____

$2\frac{1}{4}$ x $2\frac{1}{3}$ = _____

$3\frac{3}{4}$ x $3\frac{1}{2}$ = _____

$3\frac{1}{3}$ x $1\frac{1}{4}$ = _____

$2\frac{1}{6}$ x $1\frac{1}{3}$ = _____

$2\frac{1}{6}$
x $7\frac{1}{3}$

$1\frac{1}{2}$
x $6\frac{1}{4}$

$4\frac{1}{6}$ x $1\frac{2}{3}$ = _____

$2\frac{1}{6}$
x $3\frac{1}{3}$

$4\frac{3}{4}$
x $3\frac{6}{7}$

$2\frac{1}{4}$ x $2\frac{1}{6}$ = _____

$2\frac{1}{2}$ x $1\frac{1}{8}$ = _____

$4\frac{1}{2}$ x $2\frac{1}{2}$ = _____

$3\frac{1}{3}$ x $1\frac{3}{4}$ = _____

$8\frac{1}{5}$ x $1\frac{2}{3}$ = _____

$1\frac{3}{5}$
x $2\frac{3}{4}$

$2\frac{5}{8}$
x $1\frac{1}{4}$

$6\frac{5}{8}$ x $2\frac{1}{2}$ = _____

$7\frac{2}{7}$ x $1\frac{1}{2}$ = _____

$7\frac{1}{3}$ x $2\frac{2}{6}$ = _____

Solve the problems. Rename in lowest terms.

If the product is	Color the shape
greater than 0 but less than 5	yellow
greater than 5 but less than 10	orange
greater than 10 but less than 15	black
greater than 15 but less than 20	gray

Fill in the other
shapes with
colors of your
choice.

Extra! On the back of this page, use mixed numbers to write a multiplication problem
that has a product of $3\frac{1}{3}$.

Name _____

Tiptoes

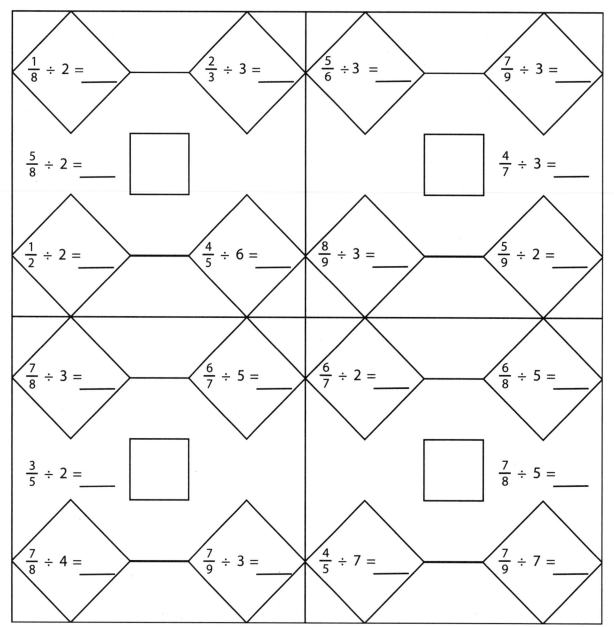

$\frac{1}{8} \div 2 =$ _____ $\qquad$ $\frac{2}{3} \div 3 =$ _____ $\qquad$ $\frac{5}{6} \div 3 =$ _____ $\qquad$ $\frac{7}{9} \div 3 =$ _____

$\frac{5}{8} \div 2 =$ _____ $\qquad$ $\frac{4}{7} \div 3 =$ _____

$\frac{1}{2} \div 2 =$ _____ $\qquad$ $\frac{4}{5} \div 6 =$ _____ $\qquad$ $\frac{8}{9} \div 3 =$ _____ $\qquad$ $\frac{5}{9} \div 2 =$ _____

$\frac{7}{8} \div 3 =$ _____ $\qquad$ $\frac{6}{7} \div 5 =$ _____ $\qquad$ $\frac{6}{7} \div 2 =$ _____ $\qquad$ $\frac{6}{8} \div 5 =$ _____

$\frac{3}{5} \div 2 =$ _____ $\qquad$ $\frac{7}{8} \div 5 =$ _____

$\frac{7}{8} \div 4 =$ _____ $\qquad$ $\frac{7}{9} \div 3 =$ _____ $\qquad$ $\frac{4}{5} \div 7 =$ _____ $\qquad$ $\frac{7}{9} \div 7 =$ _____

Solve the problems. Rename in lowest terms.

If the numerator is	Color the shape
less than 5	pink
5 or greater	purple

Fill in the other
shapes with
colors of your
choice.

 Lucy had one half of a pizza. She split it between three friends. What part of the whole
pizza did each friend get?

Name_____

Radiant Star

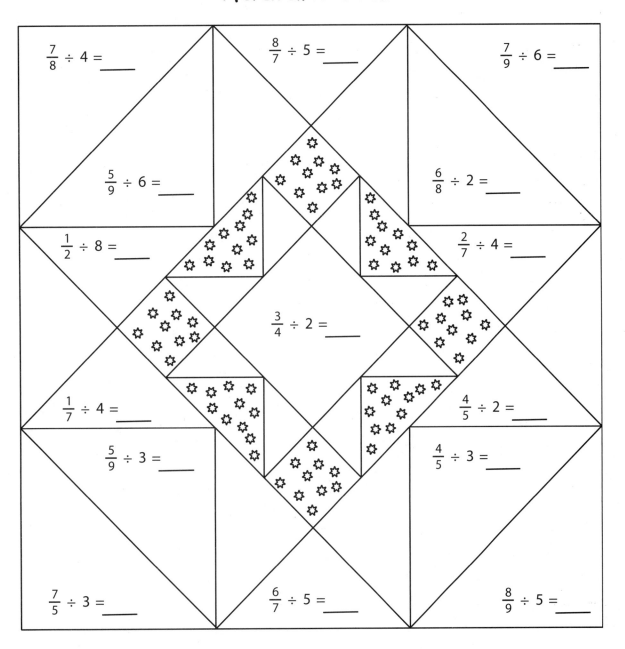

$\frac{7}{8} \div 4 =$ _____

$\frac{8}{7} \div 5 =$ _____

$\frac{7}{9} \div 6 =$ _____

$\frac{5}{9} \div 6 =$ _____

$\frac{6}{8} \div 2 =$ _____

$\frac{1}{2} \div 8 =$ _____

$\frac{2}{7} \div 4 =$ _____

$\frac{3}{4} \div 2 =$ _____

$\frac{1}{7} \div 4 =$ _____

$\frac{4}{5} \div 2 =$ _____

$\frac{5}{9} \div 3 =$ _____

$\frac{4}{5} \div 3 =$ _____

$\frac{7}{5} \div 3 =$ _____

$\frac{6}{7} \div 5 =$ _____

$\frac{8}{9} \div 5 =$ _____

On each line below, write the name of a color that you like.
Then find each quotient. Rename in lowest terms.

If the numerator is	Color the shape
less than 3	_____
between 3 and 5	_____
greater than 5	_____

Fill in the other
shapes with
colors of your
choice.

Extra! Adam cut a sheet cake into fourths. He divided each fourth into four equal pieces and
gave one to each classmate. How much of the whole cake did each person get?

Name_____

Tumbling Blocks

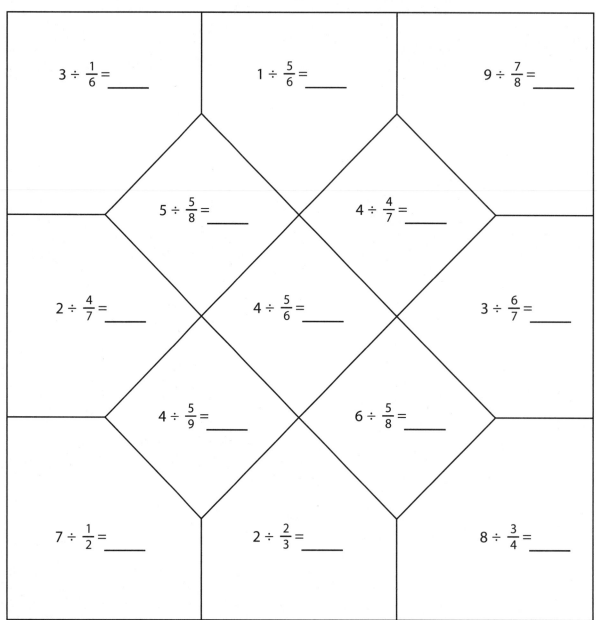

$3 \div \frac{1}{6} =$ _____

$1 \div \frac{5}{6} =$ _____

$9 \div \frac{7}{8} =$ _____

$5 \div \frac{5}{8} =$ _____

$4 \div \frac{4}{7} =$ _____

$2 \div \frac{4}{7} =$ _____

$4 \div \frac{5}{6} =$ _____

$3 \div \frac{6}{7} =$ _____

$4 \div \frac{5}{9} =$ _____

$6 \div \frac{5}{8} =$ _____

$7 \div \frac{1}{2} =$ _____

$2 \div \frac{2}{3} =$ _____

$8 \div \frac{3}{4} =$ _____

Solve the problems. Rename in lowest terms.

If the quotient is	Color the shape
less than 5	light blue
greater than 5 but less than 10	red
greater than 10	dark blue

 There are 20 sandwiches cut in half. If there is one-half of a sandwich for each student, how many students are there?

Name_____

Triangle Twister

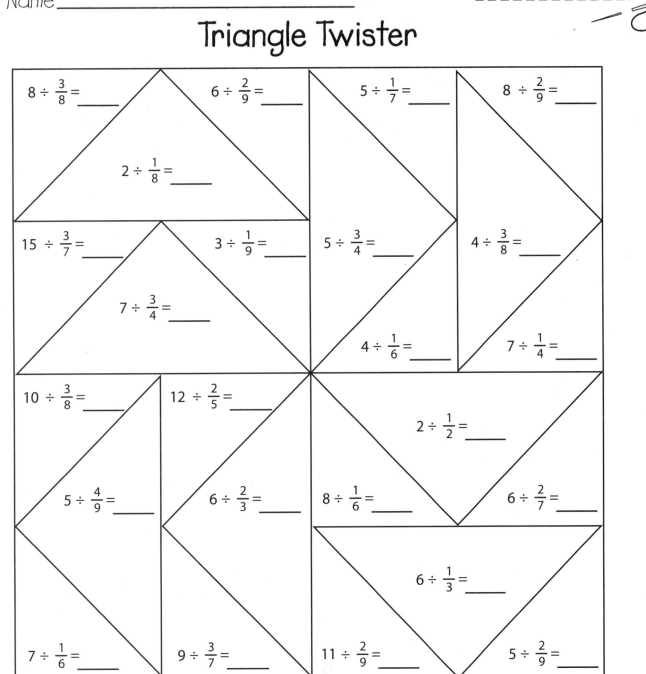

$8 \div \frac{3}{8} =$ _____

$6 \div \frac{2}{9} =$ _____

$5 \div \frac{1}{7} =$ _____

$8 \div \frac{2}{9} =$ _____

$2 \div \frac{1}{8} =$ _____

$15 \div \frac{3}{7} =$ _____

$3 \div \frac{1}{9} =$ _____

$5 \div \frac{3}{4} =$ _____

$4 \div \frac{3}{8} =$ _____

$7 \div \frac{3}{4} =$ _____

$4 \div \frac{1}{6} =$ _____

$7 \div \frac{1}{4} =$ _____

$10 \div \frac{3}{8} =$ _____

$12 \div \frac{2}{5} =$ _____

$2 \div \frac{1}{2} =$ _____

$5 \div \frac{4}{9} =$ _____

$6 \div \frac{2}{3} =$ _____

$8 \div \frac{1}{6} =$ _____

$6 \div \frac{2}{7} =$ _____

$6 \div \frac{1}{3} =$ _____

$7 \div \frac{1}{6} =$ _____

$9 \div \frac{3}{7} =$ _____

$11 \div \frac{2}{9} =$ _____

$5 \div \frac{2}{9} =$ _____

Solve the problems. Rename in lowest terms.

If the quotient is	Color the shape
less than 10	orange
greater than 10 but less than 20	yellow
greater than 20	blue

Extra! Dana has six yards of fabric to make banners. She needs one-fourth of a yard to make each one. How many banners can she make in all?

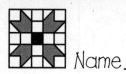

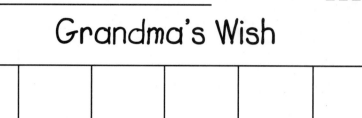

Grandma's Wish

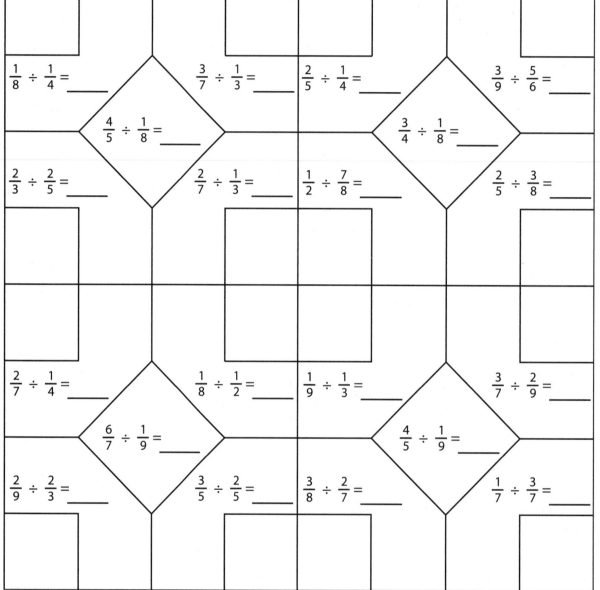

$\dfrac{1}{8} \div \dfrac{1}{4} =$ _____

$\dfrac{3}{7} \div \dfrac{1}{3} =$ _____

$\dfrac{2}{5} \div \dfrac{1}{4} =$ _____

$\dfrac{3}{9} \div \dfrac{5}{6} =$ _____

$\dfrac{4}{5} \div \dfrac{1}{8} =$ _____

$\dfrac{3}{4} \div \dfrac{1}{8} =$ _____

$\dfrac{2}{3} \div \dfrac{2}{5} =$ _____

$\dfrac{2}{7} \div \dfrac{1}{3} =$ _____

$\dfrac{1}{2} \div \dfrac{7}{8} =$ _____

$\dfrac{2}{5} \div \dfrac{3}{8} =$ _____

$\dfrac{2}{7} \div \dfrac{1}{4} =$ _____

$\dfrac{1}{8} \div \dfrac{1}{2} =$ _____

$\dfrac{1}{9} \div \dfrac{1}{3} =$ _____

$\dfrac{3}{7} \div \dfrac{2}{9} =$ _____

$\dfrac{6}{7} \div \dfrac{1}{9} =$ _____

$\dfrac{4}{5} \div \dfrac{1}{9} =$ _____

$\dfrac{2}{9} \div \dfrac{2}{3} =$ _____

$\dfrac{3}{5} \div \dfrac{2}{5} =$ _____

$\dfrac{3}{8} \div \dfrac{2}{7} =$ _____

$\dfrac{1}{7} \div \dfrac{3}{7} =$ _____

Solve the problems. Rename in lowest terms.

If the quotient is	Color the shape
less than 1	blue
greater than 1 but less than 2	red
greater than 2	yellow

Fill in the other shapes with colors of your choice.

Extra! • Find the missing fraction: _____ $\div$ $\dfrac{1}{5}$ = $\dfrac{4}{5}$

Name _____

Sweet Dreams

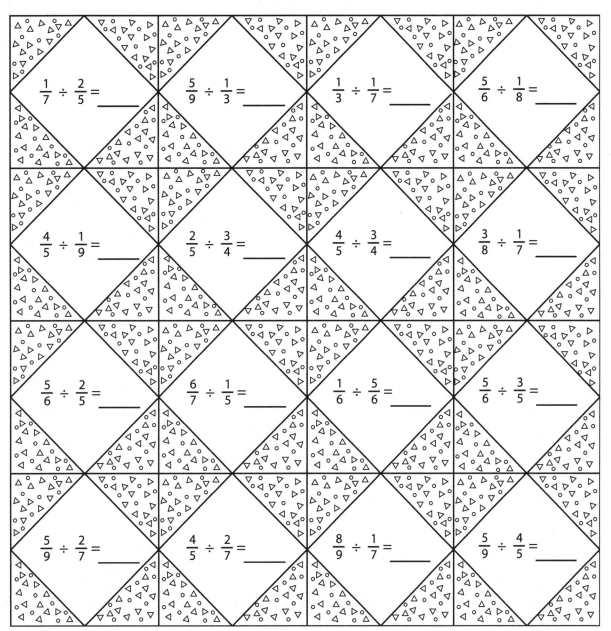

$\frac{1}{7} \div \frac{2}{5} =$ _____

$\frac{5}{9} \div \frac{1}{3} =$ _____

$\frac{1}{3} \div \frac{1}{7} =$ _____

$\frac{5}{6} \div \frac{1}{8}$ _____

$\frac{4}{5} \div \frac{1}{9} =$ _____

$\frac{2}{5} \div \frac{3}{4} =$ _____

$\frac{4}{5} \div \frac{3}{4} =$ _____

$\frac{3}{8} \div \frac{1}{7} =$ _____

$\frac{5}{6} \div \frac{2}{5} =$ _____

$\frac{6}{7} \div \frac{1}{5} =$ _____

$\frac{1}{6} \div \frac{5}{6} =$ _____

$\frac{5}{6} \div \frac{3}{5} =$ _____

$\frac{5}{9} \div \frac{2}{7} =$ _____

$\frac{4}{5} \div \frac{2}{7} =$ _____

$\frac{8}{9} \div \frac{1}{7} =$ _____

$\frac{5}{9} \div \frac{4}{5} =$ _____

Solve the problems. Rename in lowest terms.

If the quotient is	Color the shape
less than 1	pink
greater than 1 but less than 2	light green
greater than 2 but less than 3	yellow
greater than 3	light blue

Fill in the other shapes with colors of your choice.

 On the back of this page, describe in your own words how to divide by a fraction.

85

Name_____

Star Flowers

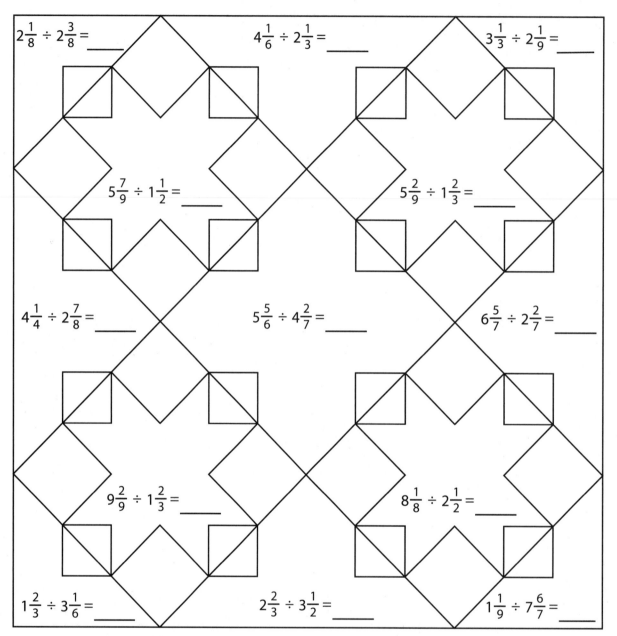

$2\frac{1}{8} \div 2\frac{3}{8} =$ _____

$4\frac{1}{6} \div 2\frac{1}{3} =$ _____

$3\frac{1}{3} \div 2\frac{1}{9} =$ _____

$5\frac{7}{9} \div 1\frac{1}{2} =$ _____

$5\frac{2}{9} \div 1\frac{2}{3} =$ _____

$4\frac{1}{4} \div 2\frac{7}{8} =$ _____

$5\frac{5}{6} \div 4\frac{2}{7} =$ _____

$6\frac{5}{7} \div 2\frac{2}{7} =$ _____

$9\frac{2}{9} \div 1\frac{2}{3} =$ _____

$8\frac{1}{8} \div 2\frac{1}{2} =$ _____

$1\frac{2}{3} \div 3\frac{1}{6} =$ _____

$2\frac{2}{3} \div 3\frac{1}{2} =$ _____

$1\frac{1}{9} \div 7\frac{6}{7} =$ _____

Solve the problems. Rename in lowest terms.

If the quotient is	Color the shape
less than 3	green
3 or greater	purple

Fill in the other
shapes with
colors of your
choice.

Extra! On the back of this page, use mixed numbers to write a division problem that
has a quotient greater than 3.

Name_____

Aztec Sun

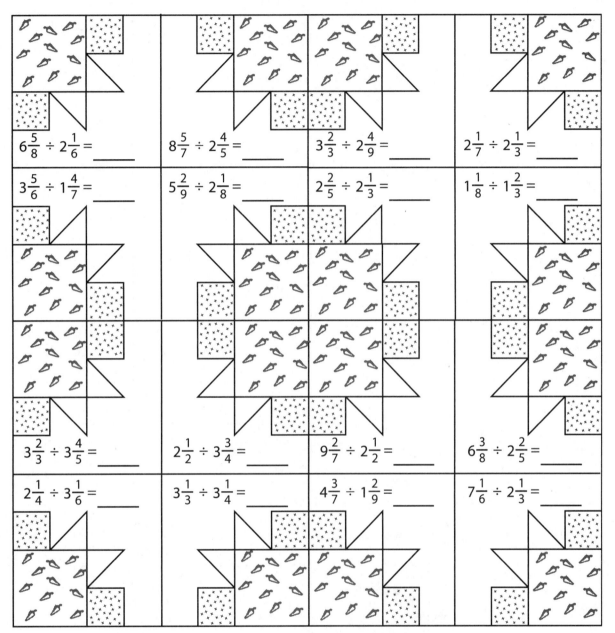

$6\frac{5}{8} \div 2\frac{1}{6} =$ _____

$8\frac{5}{7} \div 2\frac{4}{5} =$ _____

$3\frac{2}{3} \div 2\frac{4}{9} =$ _____

$2\frac{1}{7} \div 2\frac{1}{3} =$ _____

$3\frac{5}{6} \div 1\frac{4}{7} =$ _____

$5\frac{2}{9} \div 2\frac{1}{8} =$ _____

$2\frac{2}{5} \div 2\frac{1}{3} =$ _____

$1\frac{1}{8} \div 1\frac{2}{3} =$ _____

$3\frac{2}{3} \div 3\frac{4}{5} =$ _____

$2\frac{1}{2} \div 3\frac{3}{4} =$ _____

$9\frac{2}{7} \div 2\frac{1}{2} =$ _____

$6\frac{3}{8} \div 2\frac{2}{5} =$ _____

$2\frac{1}{4} \div 3\frac{1}{6} =$ _____

$3\frac{1}{3} \div 3\frac{1}{4} =$ _____

$4\frac{3}{7} \div 1\frac{2}{9} =$ _____

$7\frac{1}{6} \div 2\frac{1}{3} =$ _____

Solve the problems. Rename in lowest terms.

If the quotient is	Color the shape
less than 2	orange
2 or greater	brown

Fill in the other
shapes with
colors of your
choice.

Extra! Solve the problems. Rename in lowest terms:

$6\frac{3}{4} \div 1\frac{1}{4} =$ _____

$2\frac{1}{4} \div 3\frac{1}{3} =$ _____

Name_____

Decimals: Addition

Baby Blocks

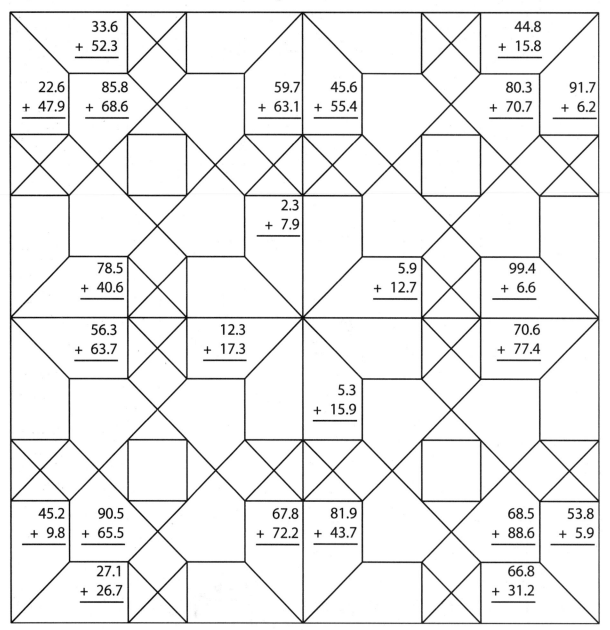

Solve the problems.

If the sum is between	Color the shape
1 and 50	pink
51 and 100	light green
101 and 150	light blue
151 and 200	yellow

Fill in the other shapes with colors of your choice.

Extra! On the back of this page, use decimals to write an addition problem that has a sum of 13.7.

88

Name _____

Tinsel Stars

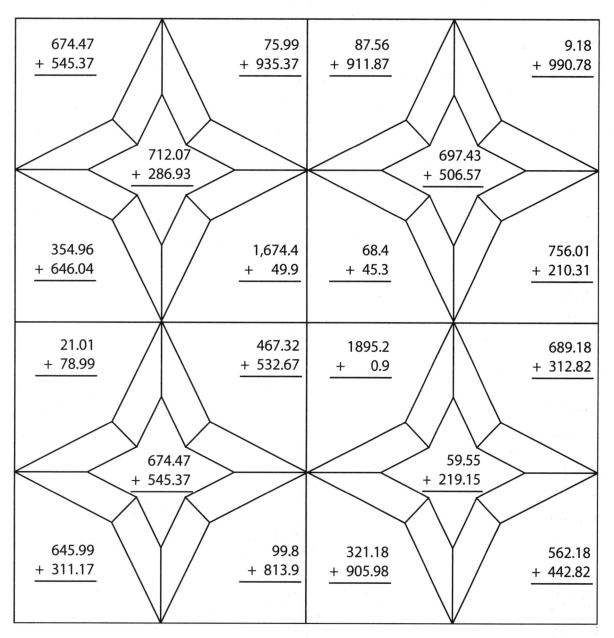

674.47
+ 545.37

75.99
+ 935.37

87.56
+ 911.87

9.18
+ 990.78

712.07
+ 286.93

697.43
+ 506.57

354.96
+ 646.04

1,674.4
+   49.9

68.4
+ 45.3

756.01
+ 210.31

21.01
+ 78.99

467.32
+ 532.67

1895.2
+   0.9

689.18
+ 312.82

674.47
+ 545.37

59.55
+ 219.15

645.99
+ 311.17

99.8
+ 813.9

321.18
+ 905.98

562.18
+ 442.82

Solve the problems.

If the sum is between	Color the shape
0 and 1000	yellow
1001 and 2000	orange

Fill in the other shapes with colors of your choice.

Extra! On the back of this page, use decimals to write an addition problem that has a whole number as its sum.

Name_____

Falling Stars

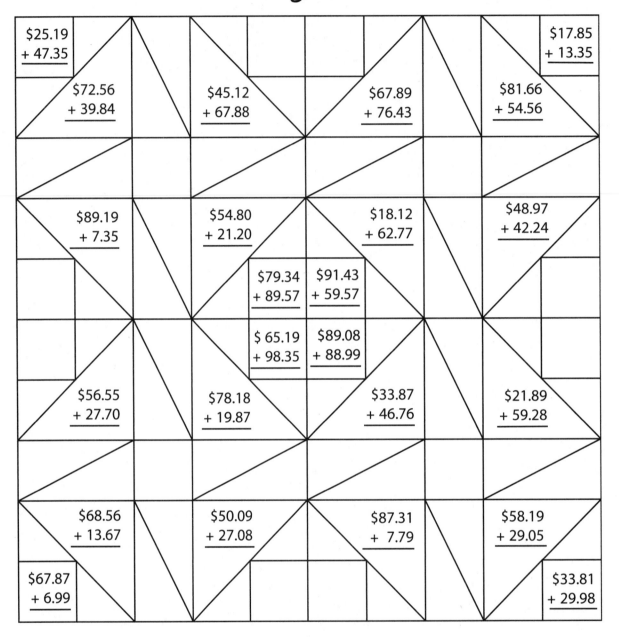

$25.19
+ 47.35

$17.85
+ 13.35

$72.56
+ 39.84

$45.12
+ 67.88

$67.89
+ 76.43

$81.66
+ 54.56

$89.19
+ 7.35

$54.80
+ 21.20

$18.12
+ 62.77

$48.97
+ 42.24

$79.34
+ 89.57

$91.43
+ 59.57

$ 65.19
+ 98.35

$89.08
+ 88.99

$56.55
+ 27.70

$78.18
+ 19.87

$33.87
+ 46.76

$21.89
+ 59.28

$68.56
+ 13.67

$50.09
+ 27.08

$87.31
+ 7.79

$58.19
+ 29.05

$67.87
+ 6.99

$33.81
+ 29.98

Solve the problems.

If the sum is	Color the shape
between $0 and $75	blue
between $76 and $150	yellow
$151 or greater	orange

Fill in the other shapes with colors of your choice.

Extra! Use mental math to decide which problem has a sum of $103.55. Circle it.

$75.15 + 27.35 = _____ $44.75 + 58.80 = _____

Sparkling Stars

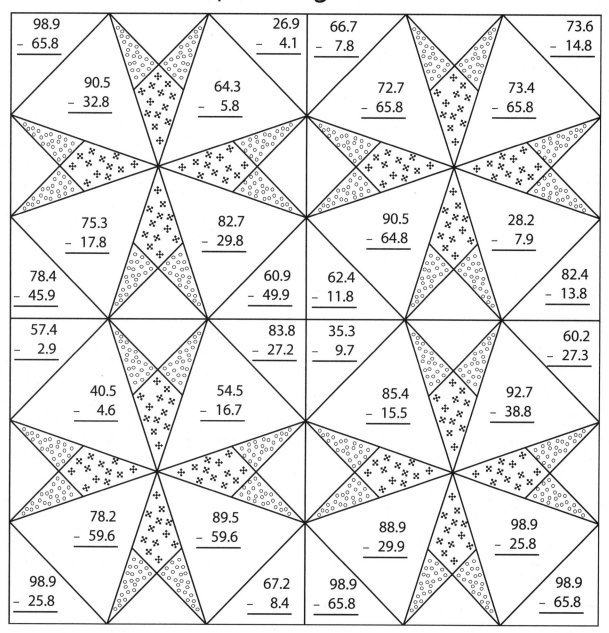

Solve the problems.

If the difference is between	Color the shape
0 and 40	orange
41 and 100	purple

Fill in the other shapes with colors of your choice.

 Extra! On the back of this page, use decimals to write a subtraction problem that has a difference of 20.9.

91

Name _____

Cousin Sherry

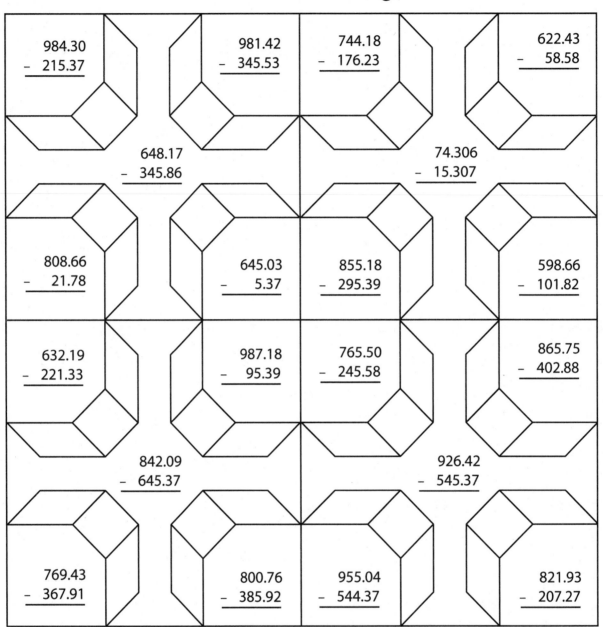

984.30
− 215.37

981.42
− 345.53

744.18
− 176.23

622.43
− 58.58

648.17
− 345.86

74.306
− 15.307

808.66
− 21.78

645.03
−   5.37

855.18
− 295.39

598.66
− 101.82

632.19
− 221.33

987.18
− 95.39

765.50
− 245.58

865.75
− 402.88

842.09
− 645.37

926.42
− 545.37

769.43
− 367.91

800.76
− 385.92

955.04
− 544.37

821.93
− 207.27

Solve the problems.

If the difference is	Color the shape
between 0 and 400	pink
401 or greater	purple

Fill in the other shapes with colors of your choice.

Extra! On the back of this page, use decimals to write a subtraction problem that has a difference greater than 800.

Name_____

Quilt Block Puzzle

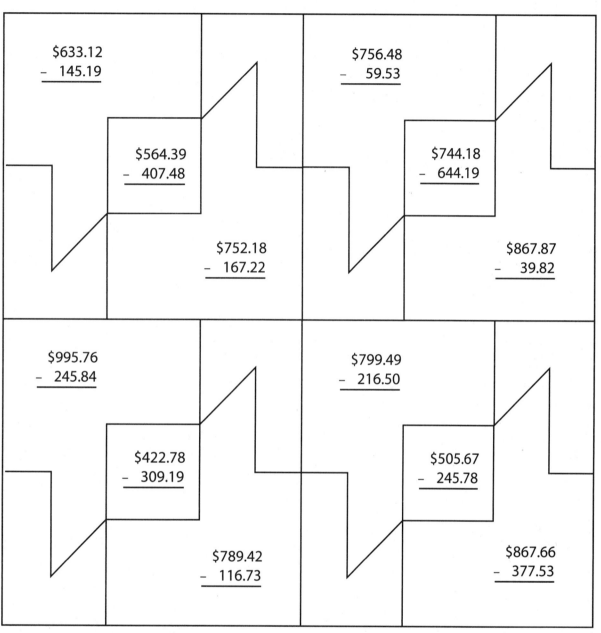

$633.12
- 145.19

$756.48
- 59.53

$564.39
- 407.48

$744.18
- 644.19

$752.18
- 167.22

$867.87
- 39.82

$995.76
- 245.84

$799.49
- 216.50

$422.78
- 309.19

$505.67
- 245.78

$789.42
- 116.73

$867.66
- 377.53

On each line below, write the name of a color that you like.
Then find each difference.

If the difference is between	Color the shape
0 and $300	_____
$301 and $600	_____
$601 and $1000	_____

Fill in the other shapes with colors of your choice.

Extra! Jia earned $892. After putting some of her money in savings, she had $758.19.
How much did she put in savings?

Name _____

Windowpane

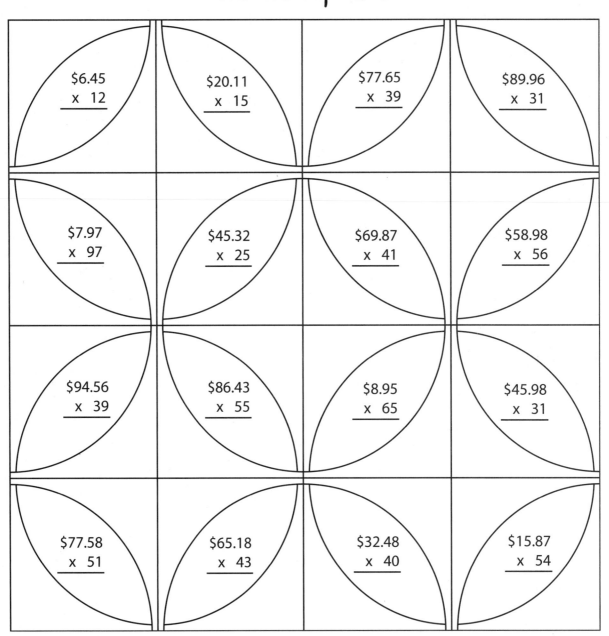

| $6.45 | $20.11 | $77.65 | $89.96 |
| x 12 | x 15 | x 39 | x 31 |

| $7.97 | $45.32 | $69.87 | $58.98 |
| x 97 | x 25 | x 41 | x 56 |

| $94.56 | $86.43 | $8.95 | $45.98 |
| x 39 | x 55 | x 65 | x 31 |

| $77.58 | $65.18 | $32.48 | $15.87 |
| x 51 | x 43 | x 40 | x 54 |

Solve the problems.

If the product is between	Color the shape
0 and $2,000	orange
$2001 and $5,000	blue

Fill in the other shapes with colors of your choice. CRAYON

 If Lance makes $8.50 an hour, how much money will he earn if he works 40 hours?

Name_____

Guiding Star

72.5 x 8			67.7 x 9	99.3 x 6			70.3 x 6
	24.3 x 8		6.82 x 3			30.9 x 6		6.97 x 9	
	50.3 x 5		0.73 x 4			0.564 x 8		99.7 x 2	
74.9 x 6			87.9 x 6	86.1 x 5			68.9 x 6
57.8 x 9			71.4 x 7	74.5 x 7			89.8 x 7
	0.687 x 8		6.55 x 7			79.9 x 4		90.7 x 4	
	78.6 x 4		77.2 x 5			29.3 x 8		9.43 x 4	
60.7 x 8			58.9 x 7				98.5 x 9

Solve the problems.

If the product is between	Color the shape
0 and 400	red
401 and 1000	purple

Fill in the other shapes with colors of your choice.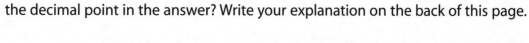

Extra! When multiplying decimals and whole numbers, how do you decide where to put the decimal point in the answer? Write your explanation on the back of this page.

Name_____

Flying Geese

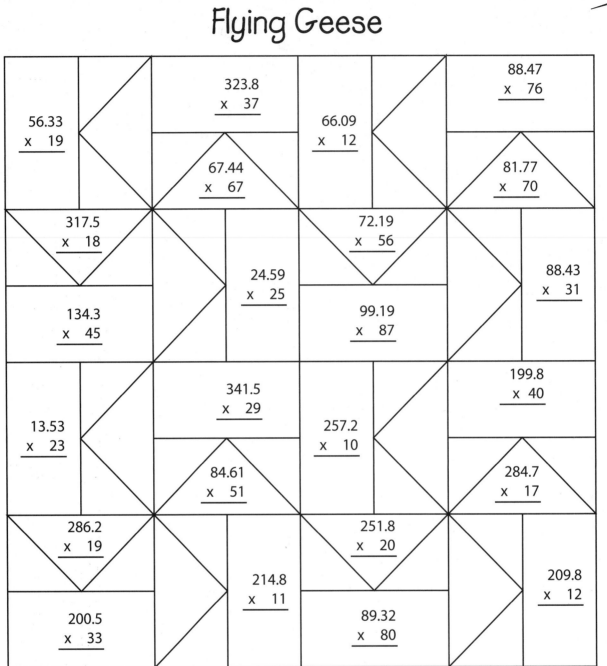

56.33
x   19

323.8
x   37

66.09
x   12

88.47
x   76

67.44
x   67

81.77
x   70

317.5
x   18

72.19
x   56

88.43
x   31

24.59
x   25

134.3
x   45

99.19
x   87

341.5
x   29

199.8
x   40

13.53
x   23

257.2
x   10

84.61
x   51

284.7
x   17

286.2
x   19

251.8
x   20

214.8
x   11

209.8
x   12

200.5
x   33

89.32
x   80

Solve the problems.

If the product is	Color the shape
between 0 and 3,000	orange
between 3,001 and 6,000	blue
greater than 6,001	green

Fill in the other shapes with colors of your choice.

Extral On the back of this page, use decimals to write a multiplication problem that has a product greater than 6,001.

Quilt Math: Grades 4–6 Scholastic Teaching Resources

Autumn Day

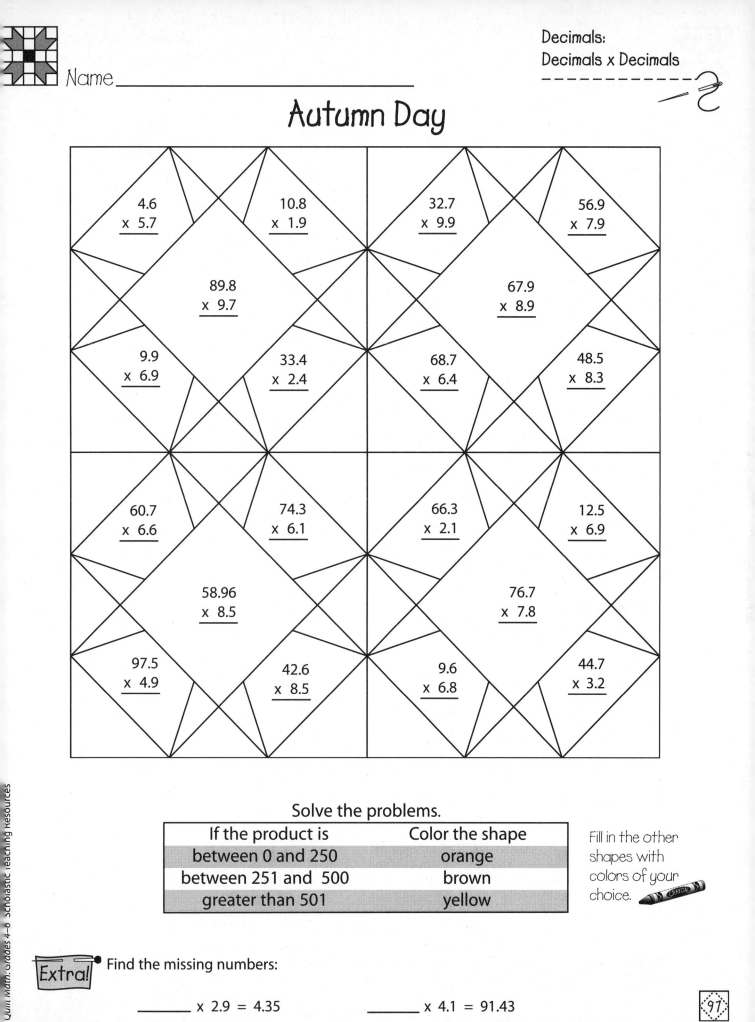

4.6
x 5.7

10.8
x 1.9

32.7
x 9.9

56.9
x 7.9

89.8
x 9.7

67.9
x 8.9

9.9
x 6.9

33.4
x 2.4

68.7
x 6.4

48.5
x 8.3

60.7
x 6.6

74.3
x 6.1

66.3
x 2.1

12.5
x 6.9

58.96
x 8.5

76.7
x 7.8

97.5
x 4.9

42.6
x 8.5

9.6
x 6.8

44.7
x 3.2

Solve the problems.

If the product is	Color the shape
between 0 and 250	orange
between 251 and 500	brown
greater than 501	yellow

Fill in the other shapes with colors of your choice.

Extra! • Find the missing numbers:

_____ x 2.9 = 4.35   _____ x 4.1 = 91.43

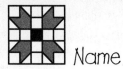

Name_____

Party Hats

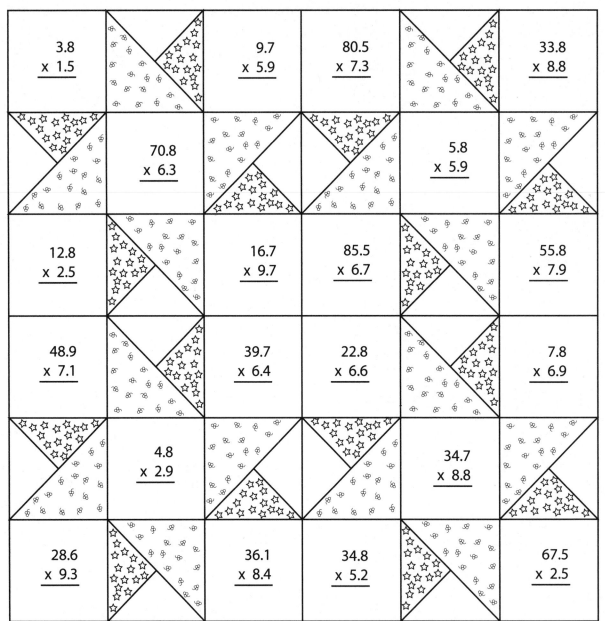

3.8 x 1.5		9.7 x 5.9	80.5 x 7.3		33.8 x 8.8
	70.8 x 6.3			5.8 x 5.9	
12.8 x 2.5		16.7 x 9.7	85.5 x 6.7		55.8 x 7.9
48.9 x 7.1		39.7 x 6.4	22.8 x 6.6		7.8 x 6.9
	4.8 x 2.9			34.7 x 8.8	
28.6 x 9.3		36.1 x 8.4	34.8 x 5.2		67.5 x 2.5

Solve the problems.

If the product is between	Color the shape
0 and 250	orange
251 and 1000	blue

Fill in the other shapes with colors of your choice.

 First estimate, then find the product: 9.7 x 4.2 = _____

98

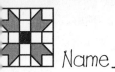

Name _____

Peaceful Hours

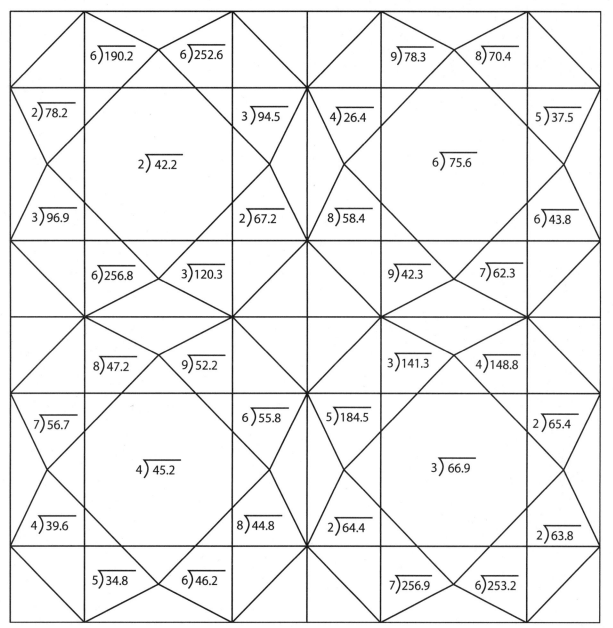

Solve the problems.

If the quotient is between	Color the shape
0 and 10	green
11 and 20	pink
21 and 30	light blue
31 and 50	yellow

Fill in the other shapes with colors of your choice.

Extra! First estimate, then find the quotient: $17.6 \div 2 =$ _____

99

Lighthouse Beacon

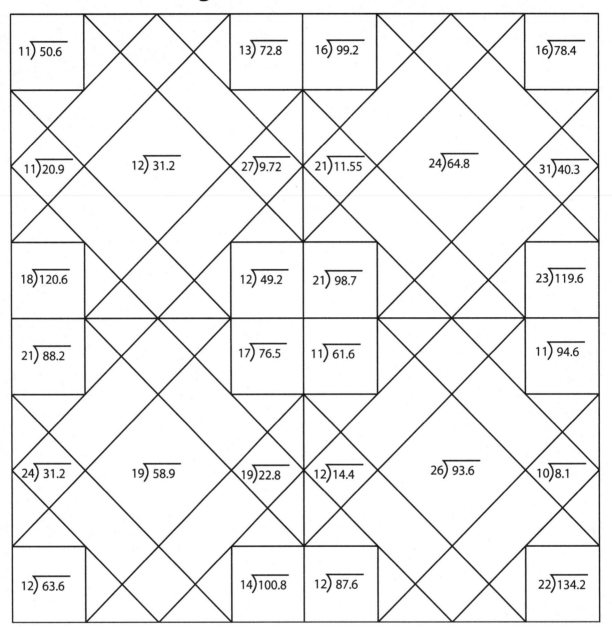

$11 \overline{)50.6}$ $13 \overline{)72.8}$ $16 \overline{)99.2}$ $16 \overline{)78.4}$

$11 \overline{)20.9}$ $12 \overline{)31.2}$ $27 \overline{)9.72}$ $21 \overline{)11.55}$ $24 \overline{)64.8}$ $31 \overline{)40.3}$

$18 \overline{)120.6}$ $12 \overline{)49.2}$ $21 \overline{)98.7}$ $23 \overline{)119.6}$

$21 \overline{)88.2}$ $17 \overline{)76.5}$ $11 \overline{)61.6}$ $11 \overline{)94.6}$

$24 \overline{)31.2}$ $19 \overline{)58.9}$ $19 \overline{)22.8}$ $12 \overline{)14.4}$ $26 \overline{)93.6}$ $10 \overline{)8.1}$

$12 \overline{)63.6}$ $14 \overline{)100.8}$ $12 \overline{)87.6}$ $22 \overline{)134.2}$

Solve the problems.

If the quotient is	Color the shape
greater than 0 but less than 2	orange
greater than 2 but less than 4	yellow
greater than 4	blue

Fill in the other shapes with colors of your choice.

Extra! Ellen bought 20 packages of hamburger buns for $79.00. How much did each package cost?

Name _____

Shoofly

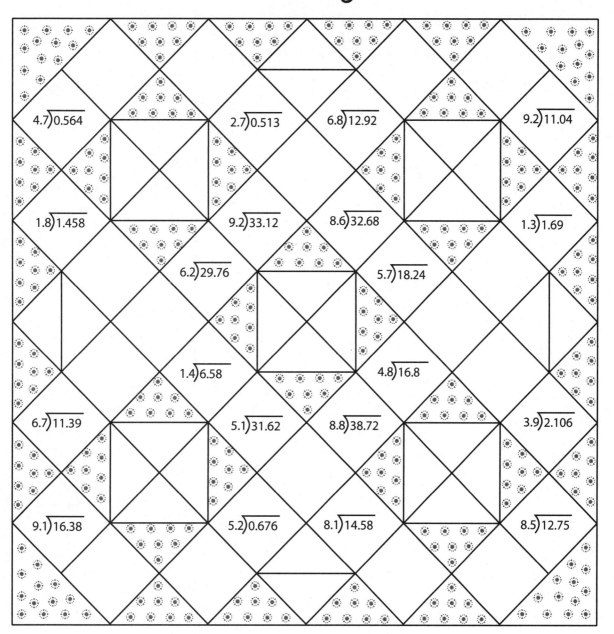

$$4.7)\overline{0.564} \qquad 2.7)\overline{0.513} \qquad 6.8)\overline{12.92} \qquad 9.2)\overline{11.04}$$

$$1.8)\overline{1.458} \qquad 9.2)\overline{33.12} \qquad 8.6)\overline{32.68} \qquad 1.3)\overline{1.69}$$

$$6.2)\overline{29.76} \qquad 5.7)\overline{18.24}$$

$$1.4)\overline{6.58} \qquad 4.8)\overline{16.8}$$

$$6.7)\overline{11.39} \qquad 5.1)\overline{31.62} \qquad 8.8)\overline{38.72} \qquad 3.9)\overline{2.106}$$

$$9.1)\overline{16.38} \qquad 5.2)\overline{0.676} \qquad 8.1)\overline{14.58} \qquad 8.5)\overline{12.75}$$

Solve the problems.

If the quotient is	Color the shape
greater than 0 but less than 2	red
greater than 2	black

Fill in the other shapes with colors of your choice.

Extra! Tamika spent $21.20 for 5.3 yards of fabric. What was the cost of each yard?

Quilt Math: Grades 4–6 · Scholastic Teaching Resources

101

Name_____

Rising Sun

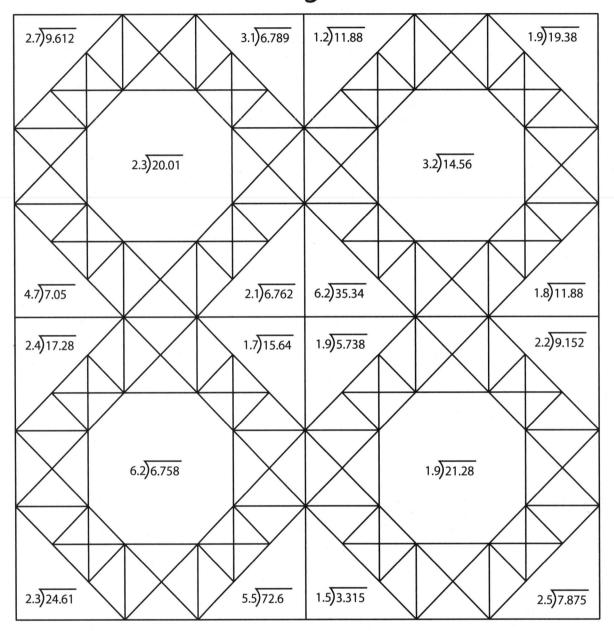

2.7)9.612   3.1)6.789   1.2)11.88   1.9)19.38

2.3)20.01   3.2)14.56

4.7)7.05   2.1)6.762   6.2)35.34   1.8)11.88

2.4)17.28   1.7)15.64   1.9)5.738   2.2)9.152

6.2)6.758   1.9)21.28

2.3)24.61   5.5)72.6   1.5)3.315   2.5)7.875

Solve the problems.

If the quotient is	Color the shape
greater than 0 but less than 5	purple
greater than 5	pink

Fill in the other shapes with colors of your choice.

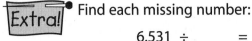 Extra! Find each missing number:

6.531 ÷ _____ = 3.11   _____ ÷ 3.9 = 1.8

Overlapping Octagons

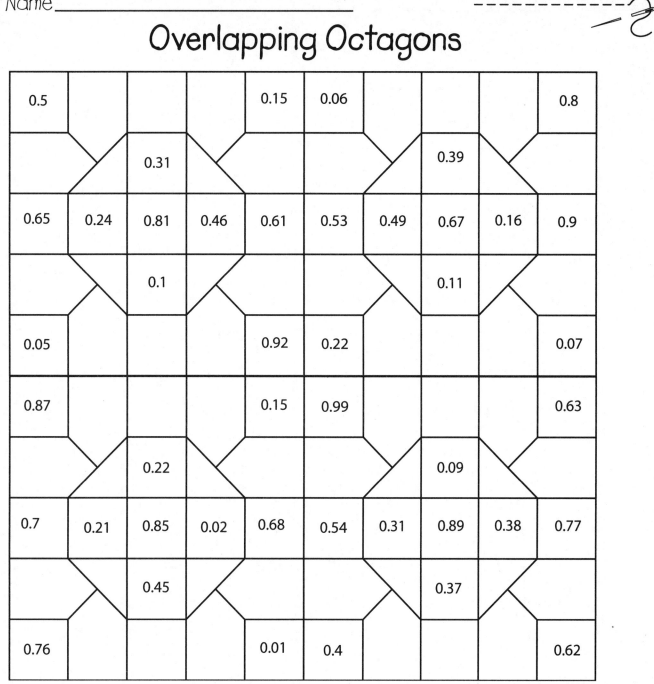

Write each decimal as a percent.

If the percent is	Color the shape
less than 50%	purple
50% or greater	orange

Fill in the other shapes with colors of your choice.

 • Express 0.05 as a percent: _____

Name _____

Illusion

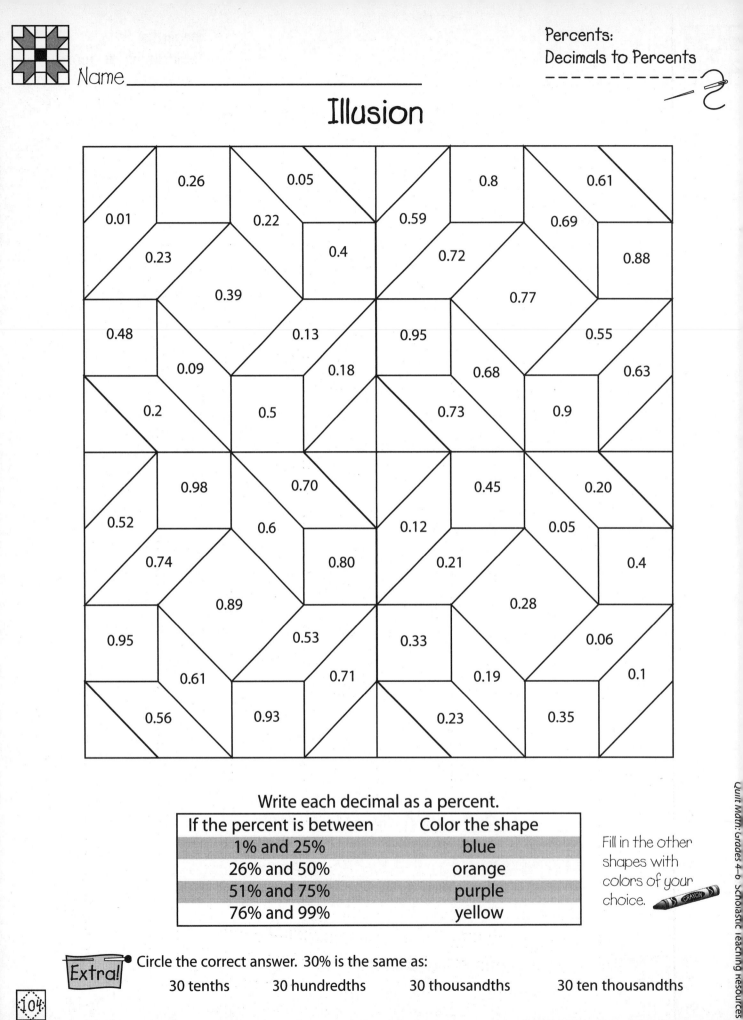

Write each decimal as a percent.

If the percent is between	Color the shape
1% and 25%	blue
26% and 50%	orange
51% and 75%	purple
76% and 99%	yellow

Fill in the other shapes with colors of your choice.

Extra! • Circle the correct answer. 30% is the same as:

      30 tenths   30 hundredths   30 thousandths   30 ten thousandths

Name_____

Busy Sidewalks

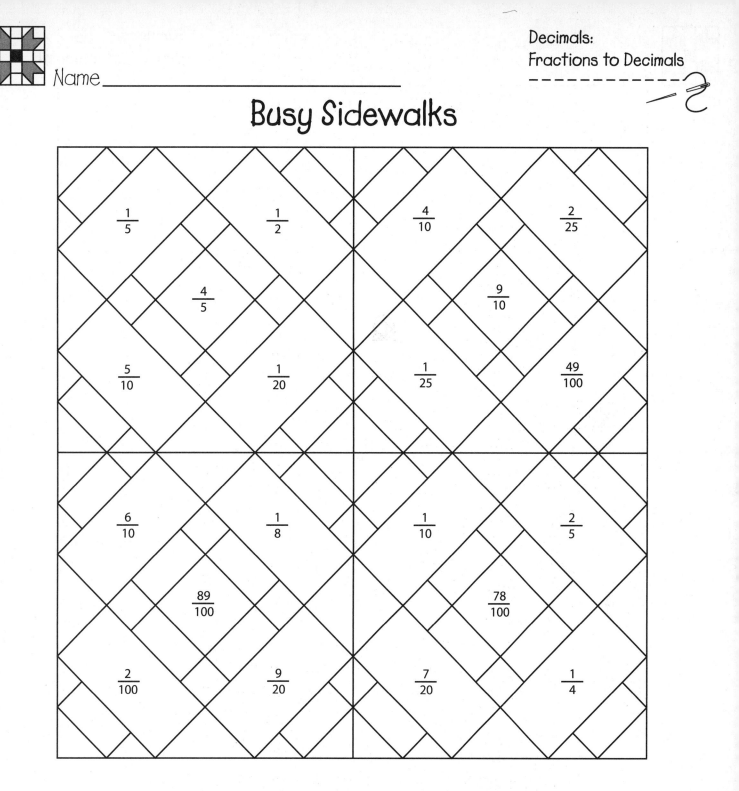

$\frac{1}{5}$ $\frac{1}{2}$ $\frac{4}{10}$ $\frac{2}{25}$

$\frac{4}{5}$ $\frac{9}{10}$

$\frac{5}{10}$ $\frac{1}{20}$ $\frac{1}{25}$ $\frac{49}{100}$

$\frac{6}{10}$ $\frac{1}{8}$ $\frac{1}{10}$ $\frac{2}{5}$

$\frac{89}{100}$ $\frac{78}{100}$

$\frac{2}{100}$ $\frac{9}{20}$ $\frac{7}{20}$ $\frac{1}{4}$

On each line below, write the name of a color that you like.
Then rewrite each fraction as a decimal.

If the decimal is between	Color the shape
0.01 and 0.33	_____
0.34 and 0.66	_____
0.67 and 0.99	_____

Fill in the other
shapes with
colors of your
choice.

Extra! Write *two-tenths* as a decimal and as a percent: _____ _____

Name _____

Interlaced Triangles

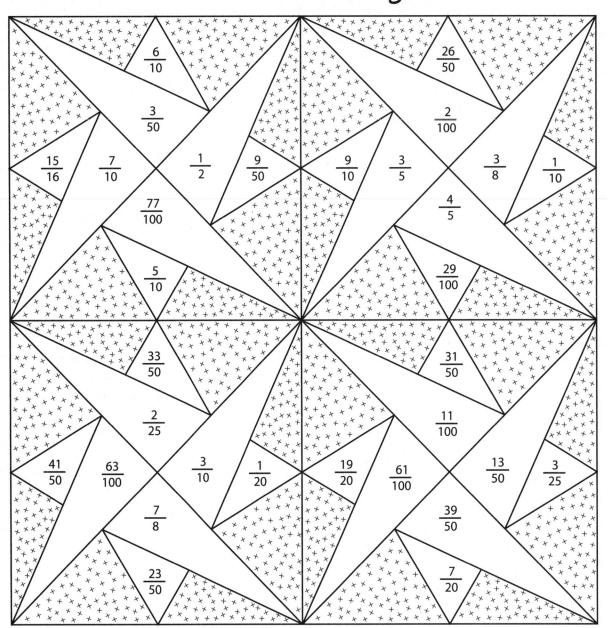

Write each fraction as a decimal.

If the decimal is between	Color the shape
0.01 and 0.25	red
0.26 and 0.50	blue
0.51 and 0.75	yellow
0.76 and 0.99	green

Fill in the other shapes with colors of your choice.

Extra! Write each fraction as a decimal rounded to the nearest hundredth:

$\dfrac{1}{6}$ $\dfrac{1}{7}$ $\dfrac{3}{9}$

Quilt Math: Grades 4–6 Scholastic Teaching Resources

Name _____

Navajo Star

Write each fraction as a percent.

If the percent is between	Color the shape
1% and 33%	orange
34% and 66%	brown
67% and 99%	yellow

Fill in the other shapes with colors of your choice.

Extra! On the back of this page, write three different fractions that are each equivalent to 50%.

Name_____

_____

(Write the name of your quilt block on the line above.)

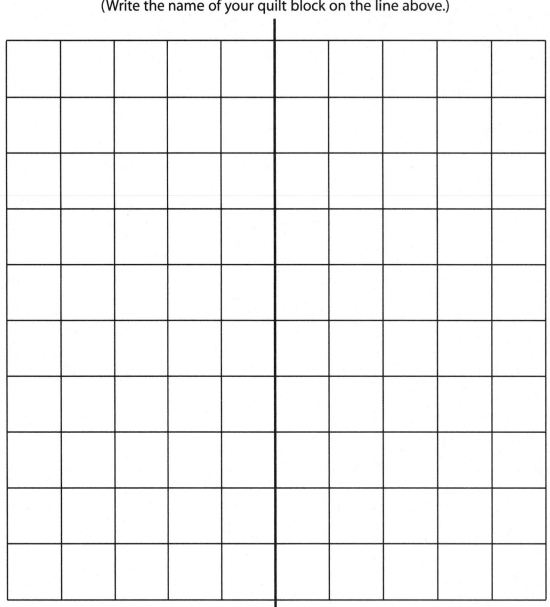

middle

On the grid, design a quilt pattern that has
vertical symmetry.

A figure, shape, or design has vertical symmetry
if the right and left sides match when you draw
a vertical line down the middle.

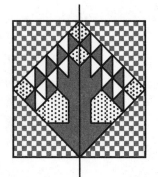

Quilt Math, Grades 4–6 · Scholastic Teaching Resources

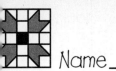

Name _____

_____
(Write the name of your quilt block on the line above.)

On the grid, design a quilt pattern that has both
vertical and horizontal symmetry.

* A figure, shape, or pattern has vertical symmetry if
  the right and left sides match when you draw a
  vertical line down the middle.

* A figure, shape, or pattern has horizontal symmetry
  if the top and bottom parts match when you draw
  a horizontal line across the middle.

Answers to the Extra! Questions

Page 8:

9,999,999

Page 9:

10,045,000

Page 10:

99,999,999,999

Page 11:

23.95

Page 12:

14.002

Page 13:

Answers will vary. Possible answers: 32,212; 32,222; 32,202

Page 14:

9,964,310

Page 15:

38.05; 38.15; 37.95

Page 16:

12.04; 12.06; 12.4; 12.44

Page 17:

30

Page 18:

Yes. 2 is a factor of 10, so any number divisible by 10 is also divisible by 2.

Page 19:

The 8 prime numbers less than 20 are: 2, 3, 5, 7, 11, 13, 17, 19.

Page 20:

13 should be circled.

Page 21:

$2^6 = 2 \times 2 \times 2 \times 2 \times 2 \times 2 = 64$

Page 22:

8^5

Page 23:

even; Answers will vary. One example: $21 + 13 = 34$

Page 24:

even; Answers will vary. One example: $32 + 44 = 76$

Page 25:

Answers will vary. Examples: $1,261 + 2,855 = 4,000$ (estimated sum); $1,798 + 2,457 = 4,000$ (estimated sum)

Page 26:

Answers will vary. Examples: $739 + 133 = 872$; $416 + 456 = 872$; $618 + 254 = 872$

Page 27:

1,022

Page 28:

Answers will vary. One example: $12,640 + 71,420 = 84,060$

Page 29:

Answers will vary. Examples: $3 + 7 = 10$; $1 + 9 = 10$; $5 + 5 = 10$; $6 + 4 = 10$; $8 + 2 = 10$

Page 30:

Answers will vary. One example: $281 + 745 = 1,026$

Page 31:

Answers will vary. One example: $932 - 388 = 500$ (estimated difference)

Page 32:

Answers will vary. One example: $879 - 125 = 800$ (estimated difference)

Page 33:

26 candles

Page 34:

$8,665 - 1,134 = 7,531$

Page 35:

18 years

Page 36:

67

Page 37:

Answers will vary. Examples: $43 - 11 = 32$; $120 - 15 = 105$; $99 - 49 = 50$

Page 38:

Answers will vary. Examples: 3×8; 6×4; 2×12

Page 39:
Answers will vary. Examples: 6 x 4 = 24; 12 x 2 = 24

Page 40:
Answers will vary. One example: 33 x 4 = 132

Page 41:
5

Page 42:
2,920 days

Page 43:
411 x 8 = 3,288

Page 44:
Answers will vary. One example: 11; 110

Page 45:
Answers will vary. One example: 42 x 11 = 462

Page 46:
145

Page 47:
125

Page 48:
Answers will vary. Examples: 48 ÷ 4 = 12; 36 ÷ 3 = 12

Page 49:
Answers will vary. Examples: 12 ÷ 3 = 4; 18 ÷ 9 = 2; 24 ÷ 4 = 6

Page 50:
8

Page 51:
If the divisor is greater than the digit in the hundreds place, the quotient will have two digits. If the divisor is less than or equal to the digit in the hundreds place, the quotient will have three digits.

Page 52:
34 ÷ 6 = 5 r. 4

Page 53:
8

Page 54:
42

Page 55:
The numbers 1 to 26.

Page 56:
$\frac{4}{5} = \frac{40}{50}$ and $\frac{2}{3} = \frac{22}{33}$ should be circled.

Pages 57:
Answers will vary. Examples: $\frac{6}{10}$; $\frac{9}{15}$; $\frac{12}{20}$

Page 58:
Answers will vary. Examples: $\frac{4}{8}$; $\frac{25}{50}$; $\frac{6}{12}$

Page 59:
$\frac{10}{12}$ should be circled.

Page 60:
26

Page 61:
Answers will vary. Examples: $\frac{9}{6}$; $\frac{15}{10}$

Page 62:
Answers will vary. Examples: $\frac{37}{5}$; $\frac{51}{8}$

Page 63:
$\frac{13}{8}$; $\frac{14}{3}$; $\frac{31}{5}$

Page 64:
Answers will vary. One example: $\frac{6}{17} + \frac{11}{17} = \frac{17}{17} = 1$

Page 65:
8

Page 66:
8

Page 67:
Answers will vary. One example: $1\frac{3}{4} + 1\frac{1}{8} = 2\frac{7}{8}$

Page 68:
Answers will vary. One example: $\frac{7}{8} - \frac{6}{8} = \frac{1}{8}$

Page 69:
Answers will vary. One example: $\frac{3}{4} - \frac{1}{2} = \frac{1}{4}$

Page 70:
Answers will vary. One example: John had one and one-half cups of sauce. He added another three and one-third cups of sauce. How much sauce did he have in all? four and five-sixth cups

Page 71:
Answers will vary. One example: $2\frac{1}{2} - 1\frac{7}{8} = \frac{5}{8}$

Page 72:
$7 \times \frac{3}{7} = 3$ should be circled.

Continued

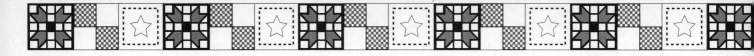

Page 73:

3; 4; 5

Page 74:

$\frac{1}{3}$ or any fraction equivalent to $\frac{1}{3}$.

Page 75:

Answers will vary. One example: $\frac{3}{7} \times \frac{1}{3} = \frac{1}{7}$

Page 76:

4

Page 77:

8

Page 78:

Answers will vary. One example: $2\frac{1}{3} \times 1\frac{1}{4} = 2\frac{11}{12}$

Page 79:

Answers will vary. One example: $2\frac{2}{9} \times 1\frac{1}{2} = 3\frac{1}{3}$

Page 80:

$\frac{1}{6}$

Page 81:

$\frac{1}{16}$

Page 82:

40 students

Page 83:

24 banners

Page 84:

$\frac{4}{25}$

Page 85:

Answers will vary. One example: To divide by a fraction, invert the divisor and multiply.

For example: $\frac{3}{4} \div \frac{3}{8} = 2$; $\frac{3}{4} \times \frac{8}{3} = 2$

Page 86:

Answers will vary. One example: $5\frac{1}{6} \div 1\frac{1}{8} = 4\frac{16}{27}$

Page 87:

$5\frac{2}{5}$; $\frac{27}{40}$

Page 88:

Answers will vary. One example: $5.8 + 7.9 = 13.7$

Page 89:

Answers will vary. One example: $321.8 + 167.2 = 489$

Page 90:

$44.75 + $58.80 = $103.55 should be circled.

Page 91:

Answers will vary. One example: $26.6 - 5.7 = 20.9$

Pages 92:

Answers will vary. One example: $987.03 - 33.12 = 953.91$

Page 93:

$133.81

Page 94:

$340.00

Page 95:

Multiply as with whole numbers. Write the product so it has as many decimal places as the sum of the decimal places in the factors.

Page 96:

Answers will vary. One example: $894.3 \times 8 = 7,154.4$

Page 97:

1.5; 22.3

Page 98:

Estimated answer is 40. Actual answer is 40.74.

Page 99:

Estimated answer is 9. Actual answer is 8.8.

Pages 100:

$3.95

Page 101:

$4 a yard

Page 102:

2.1; 7.02

Page 103:

5%

Page 104:

30 hundredths should be circled.

Page 105:

0.2; 20%

Page 106:

0.17; 0.14; 0.33

Page 107:

Answers will vary. Examples: $\frac{50}{100}$; $\frac{1}{2}$; $\frac{2}{4}$